MW01296955

PRESENT TO THE PRESENCE OF GOD:

A SHORT GUIDE TO 12 PRACTICES OF TRANSFORMING PRAYER

JON ADAMS

RIO GRANDE VALLEY. TEXAS

©2018 Jon Adams

ISBN-13: 978-1979045698

ISBN-10: 1979045690

All rights reserved - *No part of this book may be reproduced or transmitted in any form or by any means, electronic or mechanical, including photocopying, recording or by any information storage and retrieval system, without written permission from the author.*

jesusliteracy@gmail.com

Cover photo and interior diagram by the author

TO BELEN, ESTHER, AND BISONTE:

TO LETTY & MIGUEL, MELINDA & JOE, DAVID & BRYCEE, LAURA & GERARDO,
AND JIM & BEKA:

TO ADRIANA, ANNETTE, AYSSA, MATY, MITZVAH, RAYMOND, ZACH, AND
RAQUEL & MICHAEL:

AND TO ALL OF OUR FRIENDS WHO ARE PART OF OUR GBCY FAMILY, PAST,
PRESENT AND FOREVER:

THANK YOU.

CONTENTS

PREFACE 1

THE LORD'S PRAYER 7

INTRODUCTION: CHRISTIAN SPIRITUALITY AND PRAYER 9

    BIBLICAL PRAYER...12

    CHRISTIAN PRAYER..14

    HOPE VS. CERTAINTY 15

CHAPTER 1: SPIRITUAL ALIGNMENT 19

    PRACTICE 1: HOW TO PRAY FOR SPIRITUAL ALIGNMENT:............20

CHAPTER 2: MEDITATION 29

    TWO PATHS OF MEDITATION...29

    PRACTICE 2: FOCUSED MEDITATION 30

    BASIC GUIDELINES FOR MEDITATION....................................31

        MEDITATING ON SCRIPTURE I: LECTIO DIVINA.....................32

        MEDITATING ON SCRIPTURE II: IMAGINATIVE PRAYER............33

    PRACTICE 3: SILENT MEDITATION 35

        SILENT MEDITATION I: CENTERING PRAYER 37

        SILENT MEDITATION II: ABIDE/DIE/REST 39

CHAPTER 3: PRAYING WITH PRAYER BEADS 41

    HISTORY 41

    WHY BEADS?..42

    WHICH BEADS?...44

    PRACTICE 4: PRAYERS FOR BEADS 46

BEAD PRAYER I: FULL CIRCLE PRAYER...46

BEAD PRAYER II: LISTENING PRAYER 49

BEAD PRAYER III: BEADS AS A MEDITATION TIMER...................51

CHAPTER 4: BREATH PRAYERS AND MINDFUL CHORES.....................53

PRACTICE 5: BREATH PRAYERS 53

PRACTICE 6: MINDFUL CHORES...55

CHAPTER 5: PRAYING THE HOURS, PRAYER BOOKS, AND THE LITURGICAL CALENDAR
....59

PRAYER ON A SCHEDULE..59

PRACTICE 7: THE HOURS 60

PRACTICE 8: PRAYER BOOKS AND THE LITURGICAL CALENDAR 62

CHAPTER 6: LAMENT AND FASTING 65

PRACTICE 9: LAMENT..66

PRACTICE 10: FASTING..72

CHAPTER 7: SHARED SPIRITUALITY..77

PRACTICE 11: SACRED MUSIC 78

PRACTICE 12: SACRAMENT 80

BAPTISM...80

THE LORD'S SUPPER..81

CHAPTER 8: SNAKES AND TREES 85

THE FIRST SNAKE: THE PRIDE OF MYSTICAL EXPERIENCE.............86

THE SECOND SNAKE: LONELY PROPHET SYNDROME.....................89

A FINAL WORD: THE TEMPLE AND THE WIND 93

APPENDIX 1: THE PSALMS BY TYPE 99

APPENDIX 2: RESOURCES & FURTHER READING 103

ABOUT THE AUTHOR 105

"The kingdom of God is like this: a man plants seeds in the ground. He sleeps and wakes, night and day, and the seed sprouts and grows, but he doesn't know how. For the ground brings life out of herself, first the blade, then the ear, then the grain in the ear. But when the fruit is ready he harvests it, because the time of the harvest has come."

MARK 4:26-29

PREFACE

My journey deeper into prayer started about three years ago. Thanks to an excellent biblical education from childhood through college, I've always had access to great information *about* God, but the piece that I always felt was missing from my spiritual life was the full and relational joy of *knowing* God in personal experience. My spirituality was an internal conflict between a well-trained mind that needed everything about my faith rationally explained, and an underdeveloped but persistent spirit that only desired to rest daily in the presence of God. I knew the mechanics of the gospel, but had not yet experienced what Paul describes in 2 Corinthians 3:18: "We, with unveiled faces, seeing the glory of the Lord as though reflected in a mirror, are being transformed into the same image from glory to glory; this comes from the Lord, the Spirit." The spirituality of Christ-likeness and communion with God that I read about in the New Testament seemed to exist beyond all my biblical "head knowledge" and all of my church experience. It sounded like a whole lost world that I didn't have the tools to find. But I started looking anyway, pushed by the small, persistent voice of a thirsty spirit.

I read widely on human consciousness, on prayer and the Holy Spirit in Scripture, on the mystical disciplines of the historical Church, and on the practices of other religions. Prayer slowly emerged as the beating heart behind the history of all spiritual experience throughout human history. Prayer is what our brains were designed for, what makes people unique among creatures. Prayer was what we were made to do by God the Father, called to do by the Lord Jesus, and pulled to do by the Holy Spirit. By the end of my study, I knew that to experience God - and to accept my full destiny as a conscious being - I had to become a person of prayer. I also knew that I still didn't know how to pray very well, so my study continued.

Most of the Protestant books on prayer that I encountered were biblical definitions of prayer followed by reasoned arguments for its importance. Unfortunately, they contained little instruction on alternative prayer disciplines for seeking God's presence, or on how to intentionally structure a daily prayer practice for spiritual development. This didn't help. I was already convinced of the importance of prayer. What I needed was permission to explore beyond the prayer I already knew, and I needed practical advice on how to start. The older Christian traditions offered ancient prayer practices and daily routines, but I couldn't stretch my theology to justify some of their methods, like praying to the saints. I also found that many of their prayer disciplines stood only on the authority of their particular history. Perhaps this was still my mind needing everything explained rationally, but since I was seeking a fuller understanding of prayer as a concept, I needed a better reason to try out a practice than "this is just how our church does it."

In the end, I entrusted myself to God's grace and experimented with many different styles of prayer for about two years. I believe in the ever-present God in whom we "live and move and have our being,"[1] so it's hard to describe how some practices led me "closer" to God's presence while others seemed to lead me "farther" from it. Still, that was my basic experience. Some disciplines were challenging at first, but with practice proved to be the most meaningful and spiritually enlightening. Those disciplines are what I've included here. This little book is the product of a lot of trial and error, happy times and difficult times attending to the Spirit of God. I learned greatly from the works of several wise teachers, and have included the most accessible ones in Appendix 2: Resources & Further Reading at the end, which serves just as well as a bibliography. But this isn't meant to be a scholarly or academic work. I hope you'll consult the works of real prayer experts for your serious questions. My only goal here is to provide a simple resource

---

[1] Acts 17:28 (All Bible passages used are my own translation or paraphrase.)

3

to others that would have been incredibly helpful at the beginning of my journey into prayer – a resource that gives you permission to explore new concepts and practices of prayer, and straightforward advice for beginning your own prayer journey.

The most difficult thing to remember as you begin is this – prayer isn't God. Prayer is a disciplined search for communion with God, but isn't God in itself. Only God is God. We seek and pray to an Other who is real and mysterious and totally free to do whatever the Other wants. Nor are answered requests or mystical experiences the goal of prayer. Spiritual union with the Father, through Christ, in the Holy Spirit is the goal of prayer, and of the whole gospel project. The methods outlined here are not magical. They won't give you access to privileged information, or eliminate the need to learn Scripture and good theology to develop an understanding of God. They'll give you no control whatsoever over how God speaks, acts, and accomplishes the work of Christ-like transformation in your life. They are not a leash for God, they are a leash for your own soul. They are ways of being obedient, expressing gratitude, and learning to listen to what God is always doing in everything. They are the opposite of action and achievement. They are passive practices of full submission. They are ways to be still and enjoy what God has done for you in Christ, all without your help. They are ways of dying to yourself and carrying your cross daily, of crucifying your pride and paying humble attention to the Creator of everything. They are ways to decrease so that Christ will increase, and on and on. They are not about you. They are about you waking up to God.

4

You might be wondering whether or not God honors certain prayer practices over others. Some of these disciplines are strange and uncomfortable, but are they worth it? How do you know that you're honoring God, and that God will honor you? Is there a right way and a wrong way to pray?

Remember this - if God is going to work in you, it will be God who works. There is no formula to control or accelerate the process. As we'll see, to Jesus the specific practice of prayer mattered far less than the development of the spirit of prayerfulness. While alternative prayer practice might seem to some like attempts at a superior spirituality, it's really quite the opposite. All of the disciplines outlined here are nothing more than practices of humility and surrender. The only thing we do is present our whole selves, mind, body and spirit, openly and with intention to the Spirit of God. What God does and what God doesn't do from there is up to God. However, the Bible does promise that "the Lord takes pleasure in those who fear him, in those who hope in his steadfast love."[2] If these practices help you fear God and hope in his steadfast love, do them. If they frustrate you, make you uncomfortable, or play to your ego, do something else. Better still, do nothing at all.

I really believe that the grace of God is big enough to embrace every seeking heart. Seek God as you're able and trust in the grace proclaimed in the death and resurrection of Christ. This is what the Lord has always spoken to me - in Scripture, in theology, in my personal experience of life, and now in prayer. But in the practice of

---

[2] Psalms 147:11.

prayer, I hear and receive and know the grace of God *for myself* on a level that I didn't think was possible before. My prayer is that you'll find the same peace and love waiting for you in the silence of God's presence. To him be the glory forever.

Jon.

P.S. – If you're starting at the absolute beginning, the Full Circle Prayer in the chapter "Praying with Beads" is basic information on Christian prayer. Start with the first chapter, then read the sections on Praise, Confession, Supplication, and Thanks in Chapter 3. Pray this pattern with or without beads until you're ready to try something else.

THE LORD'S PRAYER

Pray then in this way:

"Our Father in heaven

Hallowed be your name

Your kingdom come

Your will be done

On earth as it is in heaven

Give us today our daily bread

And forgive us our sins

As we forgive those who sin against us

Lead us not into temptation

But deliver us from the evil one

For yours is the kingdom, the power, and the glory,

Always and forever. Amen."

INTRODUCTION: CHRISTIAN SPIRITUALITY AND PRAYER

Human spirituality is more than the religious information we claim to believe. It's our connection with everything. Internally, our spirituality includes our thoughts and attitudes about ourselves and the universe. It includes our vision of the purpose of life, and what is right and wrong to do in achieving that purpose. Outwardly, it includes our actions to relate to God and creation, to protect ourselves and others, to earn and manage resources, to express our emotions artistically, and to rest. Religious practices like going to church are spiritual experiences, but so are business transactions, sporting events, long walks, child births, family dinners, painting, shopping at the mall, watching television, and visiting the doctor.

Our spirituality is the deep reality behind our whole experience, as big as each life and as small as each breath.

Ideally, Christian spirituality brings all of these separate elements together into a unified experience of God. Communion with God is the hope and promise of our spiritual tradition. At its heart, all Christian religious learning and effort is really only seeking this one thing - sharing in the life of God.

For Christians, the first step toward unity with God is often an encounter with the Scriptures. The Bible, the sacred Word of God's worshipping community, tells a big story that deals with everything from the origins of the cosmos to our interpersonal relationships to our most secret thoughts. In every layer of the text, from the Law and the Prophets in the Old Testament to the gospels and epistles in the New, the restoration of the relationship between creature and Creator is the consistent theme. A Christian spirituality begins to develop as we read and understand the Bible's story and find ourselves in it. And our spiritual connection with God begins to heal and grow as we become aware that God's intention is always to enlighten us with a consciousness of his presence in all the things we experience in life.

The clear and definite statement of God's desire for relationship with us is the story of Jesus Christ. Jesus came as a real person to share the eternal life of God with all creatures, so that we could experience the presence of God in terms we can understand. He is "God with us," the "Word made flesh," and the "exact imprint of God's own self."[3] He came to "sum up" the whole story of God's relationship with humanity and to start it over, fresh and new and right now.[4] As we study the gospels, we learn the life, teachings, example, suffering, death, and resurrection of Christ, and encounter the heart of God through his story. An authentic encounter with Christ in Scripture soon becomes an invitation to something more. We're pulled by his story to align our spirits with his Spirit and to somehow follow his pattern of life. A truly Christian spirituality invites us to take the Bible's words about Jesus out into the world, to experience God not just by reading but by sharing in the death, resurrection, and mission of Christ, embodying him in our own times and places.

Our response to this invitation, or our alignment with the Spirit of Christ, has an inner dimension and an outer dimension. The outer dimension is our obedience to Jesus' teaching to "love your neighbor as yourself."[5] As we follow Christ's pattern of compassion, good works, and sacrifice for others, we're transformed into his image or "body" in the world.[6] The inner dimension of our response to Christ is our obedience to his command to "love the Lord your God with all your heart, soul, mind, and strength."[7] Loving God with our strength is almost always interpreted by Jesus as working to bless other human beings in tangible ways with our efforts and resources. The command to love God with our hearts, souls, and minds, however, is

---

[3] Matthew 1:23; John 1:14; Hebrews 1:3.
[4] Ephesians 1:10.
[5] Matthew 22:39; Leviticus 19:18.
[6] 1 Corinthians 12:27.
[7] Matthew 22:37; Deuteronomy 6:5.

a command to love God by having our inner reality transformed into the image or Spirit of Christ. The apostle Paul described this experience as "beholding in a mirror the face of the Lord" and being "transformed into his image from glory to glory."[8] The beholding of Christ that changes our inner reality is a spiritual discipline that begins with the practice of daily reading, meditation, and prayer.

BIBLICAL PRAYER

Jesus taught us not to "heap up empty phrases like the unbelievers do, for they think they will be heard by their many words. Do not be like them, for your Father knows what you need before you ask him."[9] When he said this, he was drawing on the long biblical tradition of personal intimacy with God. The God of the Bible isn't an object or a force that can be manipulated to get what we need, although that's where the idea of prayer stops for too many of us. The God Jesus knew as Father is the God who is emotionally engaged in the lives of his children. God is a Person, and when we're aware that he's alive and free to speak for himself our relationship with him opens into an interpersonal one. Instead of approaching him with endless rituals and demands, the biblical hope in God as a Person invites us to relate to him as we ought to relate to others – by listening to him and loving him in response to his love for us.

The Preacher of Ecclesiastes writes, "Be careful how you approach the house of God. Drawing near to listen is better than offering the sacrifice of fools, for they don't even know that they're

---

[8] 2 Corinthians 3:18.
[9] Matthew 6:7-8.

doing evil. Do not be quick with your mouth, or let your heart be in a hurry to speak before God, for God is in heaven and you are on earth – so let your words be few."[10] This attitude of listening and reverence is the distinctive biblical spirituality of communion with God. Throughout the Bible, prayer is always much more of a consistent spiritual openness to God's presence than a list of requests or demands. Biblical prayer is a spiritual alignment with the Spirit of God that gives God the first word in communication to us and the last word in our response to him. As hard as it is to believe, biblical prayer actually allows for real conversation with the Creator of the Universe.

Yet conversation with God is unlike any other communication we will ever experience, and the biblical examples of it are incredibly diverse. Throughout the Bible, God's people were often moved to fast, some for weeks at a time. Many of them experienced God on lonely desert mountaintops, others through God's revelation in nature, and others through formal religious rituals, prayer, and community worship. Adam and Eve, Moses, Samuel, and Elijah simply talked to God.[11] Cain, Abraham, and Moses argued with God. Jacob physically wrestled with the angel of the Lord. David and the other psalmists wrote songs of soaring joy and terrible heartbreak. The blood of Abel and the nation of Israel cried out against injustice. Isaiah, Ezekiel, Jeremiah, Daniel, several minor prophets, Peter, Paul, and John all had terrifying visions that shook their

---

[10] Ecclesiastes 5:1-2.
[11] Exodus 33:11.

understanding of reality. At Pentecost the apostles were possessed by the Holy Spirit as they prayed, driven out into the streets to preach. Abraham, Isaac, Hannah, Elijah, Daniel, and Jesus took time to sit in silence and seek God in restful meditation. There are 650 different prayers listed in the Bible, and most of them were prayed in their own unique style and form.[12] Yet in all biblical prayer, intimacy with the God, not specific religious routines or practices, seems to be the common approach to the Creator. However we do it, showing up in prayer to relate to the Living God is all that actually seems to matter.

CHRISTIAN PRAYER

Thankfully the practice of *Christian* prayer – the New Testament communion with God that transforms our inner selves into the image of Christ – was taught in simple terms by Jesus himself, and to regular people. Matthew 6:1-18, Luke 11:1-13, and Luke 18:1-14 are some of the major collections of Jesus' teaching on prayer, although there are others. Jesus, in continuity with the biblical tradition, saw prayer as a function of our inner reality and our personal intimacy with God, so his instruction avoids prescribing specific methods or rituals. Instead, Jesus works to create a *spirit of prayerfulness* in the hearts of his disciples that represents a proper understanding of who God is and who we are in relation to him. The teaching and example of Jesus reveal at least 6 core attitudes that make up the heart of prayerfulness: humility, sincerity, privacy, creativity, persistence, and receptivity. As long as we follow Jesus' guidance into a spirit of

---

[12] Herbert Lockyer, *All The Prayers of the Bible* (Zondervan, 1990).

prayerfulness, the forms and rituals of our prayers are left open for experimentation and adaptation. There's no wrong way to pray, if we approach God personally and with reverence in a spirit of prayerfulness.

HOPE VS. CERTAINTY

Before we go any further - how can we be sure that God even hears our prayers? How can we know that his Spirit is present in our prayer practice? How can we be confident that our personal method is the "right" way to pray?

The Christian faith is a spirituality of hope, not certainty. We don't pray to idols that we can make or control, but to the infinite, mysterious Source of Life that sustains and animates the universe. We don't practice specific religious rituals to guarantee reliable responses from God. Instead we live, love, and pray in the simple hope that God is present, that God speaks, and that he cares about little creatures like us. In strictly human terms, we don't *know* that this is true at all, but we do *believe* that it is, and live our lives accordingly.

Adults, with all of our fears and worries, have to know the outcomes of things for certain before we invest our time or effort. We have so many people to care for, to protect, and to please that we're naturally suspicious of anything that might be a waste of time. People depend on us, and we don't have a lot of room in our lives to take chances or risk mistakes. In other words, we don't have much space for hope.

Jesus calls us away from certainty and back to hope by calling us out of adulthood and back into child-likeness.[13] He says "Unless you change and become like little children, you will never enter the kingdom of God."[14] This isn't an invitation to be irresponsible, or a denial that there are people who depend on us. This is a reminder that we're God's children and he's our Father. We depend on him, he doesn't depend on us. He knows for certain, we're allowed to hope. He works to provide and protect, we get to play and fall down and experience new things.

On the inner spiritual journey, our hope is that God will honor any honest, humble attempt for intimacy with him. Our hope is that God will forgive our mistakes as we stretch our souls in new directions and experience new practices of prayer. Our hope is that the Holy Spirit will translate our imperfect effort into something that is pleasing to God, always guiding us back home to his presence and his heart.[15] And our hope is that, at least in this one area of our inner lives, God has given us the grace to laugh and play and make mistakes – that he has given us the grace to be children again. He's our heavenly Father, and Fathers don't destroy their children when they make mistakes.[16] The worst thing – and the best thing! – that will happen if our methods of prayer miss the mark is that the Spirit of God will discipline us by correcting our posture, straightening our aim, and teaching us to shoot better. This is a function of God's love

---

[13] Not childishness, of course, which is exemplified by selfishness, but child-likeness which is exemplified by a sense of wonder.
[14] Matthew 18:3.
[15] Romans 8:26-27.
[16] See Psalm 103.

and his desire for full communion with his children. In the end it's up to God whether or not he hears our prayers or honors our practices. So we practice prayer, loosely and even playfully, as a discipline of hope in God.

CHAPTER 1: SPIRITUAL ALIGNMENT

Before you start any sort of daily prayer practice, it would be helpful to reflect on the spirit of prayerfulness taught by Jesus. There are 6 spiritual attitudes listed here, so a good option would be to go through them, one each day, for a week. Even if you don't take a week to do this exercise, at least read through each attitude to become familiar with it. It's important to align your heart with Christ before you move on to other practices, since the spirit of prayer matters much more to God than the form of it.

PRACTICE 1: HOW TO PRAY FOR SPIRITUAL ALIGNMENT:

1. Share your desire with God for a restored relationship of life and unity with him.

2. Spend some time each day reading the Bible passages and reflecting on the spiritual attitudes that Jesus taught.

3. Consider how Christ, as a human being like you, embodied each attitude in his life, death, and resurrection.

4. Confess your weaknesses in each area to God, and ask for the help and guidance of the Holy Spirit to be transformed into the image of Christ.

5. Pray the short prayer at the end of each section several times throughout the day, or feel free to create your own. The idea is to live in awareness of each spiritual attitude.

6. On the seventh day, review the 6 attitudes and ask God to guide the next step of your inner journey toward intimacy with him.

DAY 1: HUMILITY – LUKE 18:10-14

In Luke 18:10-14, Jesus tells a story about a religious official and a tax collector, the two opposite extremes of religious devotion in his time. The tax collector, representing everyone who we see as unworthy, humbly prays "God, have mercy on me, a sinner." His prayer is honored by God, while the religious official's self-righteous bluster is not. Jesus teaches that prayer requires a total shift in perspective, away from boasting of our own worth in order to force God into giving us what we want. When we try to manipulate God, even through good behavior, we insult his essential mystery and ignore his freedom to act as he pleases. But when we feel unworthy of God, we judge ourselves instead of letting God be the God who forgives and invites us to relate to him. True prayer moves toward perfect humility, and humility means letting go of our judgments of worthiness, pride, and desires. It means recognizing that God is God and we're not, and that we're totally dependent on him. And it means placing all of our hope on God's grace and mercy to forgive and to restore his relationship with us himself.

The mercy prayer of the tax collector, along with the prayers of many other disenfranchised characters in the gospels, is the biblical foundation for one of the church's great historical prayers, the *Kyrie Eleison* ("Lord have mercy" in Greek). The Jesus Prayer, the Eastern Orthodox version of the prayer, is "Lord Jesus Christ, Son of God, have mercy on me, a sinner." It's repeated at many times during the day by Orthodox Christians, and is a model of what it means to be humble before God.

PRAYER: *Father God, the Lord Jesus humbled himself to become like me and to die on a cross; send your Spirit to teach me how to let go of my pride and to live humbly in your love and peace. Amen.*

DAY 2: SINCERITY — MATTHEW 5:1-12

Only the humble can be truly sincere. When all pride has been crucified, the need to lie or to make more of ourselves than what we are dies with it. With God, trying to hide our true motives and feelings is useless anyway. Jesus taught that "everything that is concealed will be brought to light and made known."[17] God already knows the feelings and intentions of each heart, and to acknowledge his presence even in our sinfulness is at the core of the spirit of prayerfulness. Sincerity is openness, and only in complete openness can we experience full communion with God. It takes courage to be open about our weaknesses, and to admit that we're powerless to hide from God's sight, but this openness is also a sign that we've learned to trust the God who hears our prayers.

Sincerity in prayer is also our real, conscious presence with God in the moment. It means eliminating distractions and hidden motives, and committing our full selves to what we're praying. It means being truly conscious of the presence and communicating attention of God. Sincerity in prayer is purity of intention, effort, and awareness, and maintaining consistent sincerity is just as difficult as it sounds.

PRAYER: *Father God, in death the Lord Jesus fully committed his spirit into your hands; send your Spirit to teach me to trust you with my whole self, to live sincerely and openly in your love and peace. Amen.*

DAY 3: PRIVACY – MATTHEW 6:5-6

Jesus consistently condemns religious rituals, and even charity, when they are performed to receive the praise of human beings. The same is true of prayer: "When you pray, go into your room, close the door and pray to your Father, who is unseen. Then your Father, who

---

[17] Luke 8:17.

sees what is done in secret, will reward you."[18] True intimacy in any human relationship is never public, nor is our intimacy with God supposed to be for public display. Every temptation to boast or flaunt our prayer achievements for the admiration of others must be resisted. Prayer's reward isn't human praise but knowing God and being known by him. Nor can spiritual practice ever be a means to control others. Any insight or conviction received in prayer is almost always an exclusive gift from God to the person praying, and isn't meant to be forced onto other people. Privacy is also protection. If you keep your prayer practice between you and God, you'll never find yourself trying to explain or defend your spirituality to others. This is especially helpful with those who are suspicious of your practice of inner communion with God because they don't understand prayer beyond simply asking for things.

PRAYER: *Father God, the Lord Jesus rejected the praise of people and remained purely committed to your will; send your Spirit to teach me to live privately and intimately in your love and peace. Amen.*

DAY 4: CREATIVITY – MATTHEW 6:7-15

The "Lord's Prayer" or "Our Father" in Matthew 6:7-15 is a brilliant and truly creative prayer that addresses every aspect of human spiritual life. And it's short. Jesus takes us from praise to petition to confession to intercession and back to praise in only 12 lines and with simple words. There is no need to learn any holy vocabulary or fancy forms. True prayer as taught by Christ requires

---

[18] Matthew 6:6.

perfect soul, not perfect skill. The communication of prayer is from spirit to Spirit and back again, and doesn't require magic words, advanced intelligence, or the analytical mind. We're free to pray as we feel, and to trust that God will hear us even when our prayers are short on words. It's a great help to study the Lord's Prayer and understand all the heart and soul that Jesus pours into just a few simple lines. True depth of meaning without useless decorations is the creative style of Jesus' prayer. The test of prayer is not its art but how much of our souls we can commit to modest ideas.

PRAYER: *Father God, you created the whole universe through Christ with just a few words; send your Spirit to teach me your creativity, to pour my heart and soul into the simple rhythms of your love and peace. Amen.*

DAY 5: PERSISTENCE – LUKE 11:5-8, 18:1-8.

Jesus tells two stories about staying persistent with prayer - the parable of the widow and the unrighteous judge, and the parable of your neighbor waking you up to borrow bread in the middle of the night. In both stories, imperfect human beings (the judge and you) meet the needs of someone whom they would rather not help because of their persistence. This is a contrast between us and God, who always listens to our prayers, freely gives good gifts to every creature every day, and loves us deeply as a perfect Father loves his children. The teaching in these parables isn't that we have to work hard to get God's attention, as other people might have to do with us. It's that intimacy with God develops over time. His transforming

Spirit is poured out on anyone who persistently asks.[19] God works in people who show up, who are consistent and faithful in their spiritual openness to him. The fully developed spirit of prayerfulness is described by Paul as praying "in the Spirit at all times and on every occasion."[20] Of course that's impossible, unless we fight to include prayer in our daily rhythm and persistently ask for God's help.

PRAYER: *Father God, the Lord Jesus did not abandon us even when the world turned against him; send your Spirit to teach me in all circumstances to live persistently in love and peace with you. Amen.*

DAY 6: RECEPTIVITY

Many of us miss God's work in our lives because he doesn't answer our prayers exactly as we imagine he should. Or by the time he works, our anxious hearts have already moved on to new cares and worries and we completely overlook his blessing. But Jesus taught that the God who hears our prayers gives us what we need when we need it, and that's also true for his gift of the Holy Spirit.[21] The real trick is to recognize it when it happens.

Paul prayed that God would bless the people in his churches with "power through his Spirit in your inner being, so that Christ may dwell in your hearts through faith" and that "with all the saints you may have strength to understand what is the breadth and length and height and depth, and to know the love of Christ that surpasses all knowledge, that you may be filled with all the fullness of God."[22]

---

[19] Luke 11:13,
[20] Ephesians 6:18.
[21] Luke 11:11-13.
[22] Ephesians 3.

Those are bold requests! Yet too many of us approach prayer as a method to make God do something fleeting and external. The spirit of prayerfulness is the discipline of being internally receptive to what God is already doing, in us and in the rest of creation, often at a level much deeper than our material needs. With Paul we ask for enlightenment, to have the "eyes of our hearts" opened to see the work and blessing of God in all things.[23] We die to ourselves, our worries, and desires, and learn to trust that God is working things toward his own goals in his own way and on his own schedule. We pray for help and blessing, but we sit in faith and wait for God to move, hoping and praying that we will recognize and understand it when he does. And in our inner practice of contemplating Christ, we believe that God will actually speak to us through his Spirit, his Word, and his Son. Receptivity means that we're aware and open to the reality of God beyond ourselves, that we understand that God is Someone Else and that we need his help to recognize his communication to us. True receptivity will open our eyes to what God has been doing the whole time.

PRAYER: *Father God, the Lord Jesus prayed, "Not my will but yours be done;" send your Spirit to teach my heart to be open to all of your words and work, and to live receptively in your love and peace. Amen.*

The rest of the spiritual disciplines in this book are simply different ways of entering the spirit of prayerfulness that Jesus taught. Some of these practices will speak to you, while others might

---

[23] Ephesians 1:18.

make you uncomfortable. Be creative, take what works for you and ignore what doesn't. Remember that everything we do in prayer is about showing up to be remade in Christ's image and to experience the life of God that he desires to share with us. As Jesus taught, "Blessed are the pure in heart, for they will see God."[24] Keep your intentions and your heart pure, and in a spirit of prayerfulness "draw near to God and he will draw near to you."[25]

---

[24] Matthew 5:8.
[25] James 4:8.

CHAPTER 2: MEDITATION

TWO PATHS OF MEDITATION

Meditation is common to all religions, though we practice it in many different forms. While this is probably an oversimplification, there are two basic paths of meditation – the path of intense focus on a concept or idea, and the path of emptiness and openness to a reality beyond ourselves. The most ancient biblical tradition of meditation allows for both paths - Psalm 1:2 speaks blessing on the man who delights in the Law of the Lord and "meditates on it day and night," while Psalm 46:10 teaches us to "be still and know that I am God." The Christian tradition of the New Testament also teaches both paths. Paul instructs us in Colossians 3:1-2 to "strive for heavenly things… set your mind on things above, not on earthly things." Yet he also teaches in Galatians 2:20 that his old self has been "crucified with Christ; it is no longer I who live, but Christ who lives in me." In Christian spirituality, the path of focused attention and the path of silent surrender both have their place, and both work together to lead us toward transformation into the image of Christ.

PRACTICE 2: FOCUSED MEDITATION

Jewish and Christian spiritual practices have always been centered on the Book. We believe that the Bible is a God-inspired communication of spiritual reality, and intense concentration on Scripture has been the most common meditation practice for God's historical community. Moses instructed the people of Israel to live in constant awareness of the words of God by teaching the Law to their children, binding it on their hands and foreheads, and writing it on the gates and doorposts of their homes.[26] *Hagah*, a Hebrew word translated as "meditate" in the Old Testament, means to mutter, mumble, groan, or growl. It represents the ancient practice of repeating passages of Scripture over and over again in a low, quiet voice to focus the attention of the mind and uncover the multiple layers of meaning in each text. In the New Testament, James instructs his church not just to read the Bible but to "receive the word implanted in you, which is able to save your souls."[27] We also know that the apostles meditated deeply on the Old Testament to better understand Christ's fulfillment of God's ancient promises to the Hebrew prophets and to understand the full mystery of Christ's

---

[26] Deuteronomy 6:1-9.
[27] James 1:21.

30

cross.[28] Meditation on Scripture for true spiritual experience and transformation is as old as the oldest biblical traditions.

Regular, focused meditation on God and his Word is incredibly helpful for our spiritual development. It slows our minds and eliminates distractions so that the Spirit can bring our attention to what God wants to show us in each passage. It also takes the text from the level of information or "head knowledge" and brings it into our personal experience of life. We might know from Scripture that "those who call on the name of the Lord will be saved,"[29] but when you meditate on those words, your heart becomes aware that they are about *you*, right now. Correct biblical information expands the horizons of our knowledge of God, but simply knowing God's truth isn't all that sharing his life involves. David writes that God desires "truth in the innermost being" and teaches us wisdom in the "secret heart."[30] At some point we have to appropriate God's word for ourselves, let it work in us, and allow our souls to respond. Over time, the Spirit uses meditation on Scripture to transform your soul and make you aware that God's truth is true about you.

BASIC GUIDELINES FOR MEDITATION

In all meditation it's important to set aside a time and place where you can pray in silence and privacy. Children, spouses, cellphones, exhaustion, and other interruptions will frustrate you and make it hard to stay persistent in your practice. There is no space for

---

[28] See Ephesians 3:1-10.
[29] Joel 2:32, Acts 2:21, Romans 10:13.
[30] Psalm 51:5-6.

meditation in the daily routine until you make it. It will be a struggle, especially at the beginning.

In Christian meditation, no special posture or equipment is required. Sit comfortably, but not so comfortably that you'll fall asleep. In most forms, no special breathing rhythm is required either, so let your body relax. Let go of the weight and tension of the past, and let the future worry about itself. Try to bring your attention to what you're doing in the present moment, because the present moment is where we encounter God.

MEDITATING ON SCRIPTURE I: LECTIO DIVINA

Guigo, a 12th century Carthusian monk, described a system of spiritual engagement with Scripture that he called *Lectio Divina* or "holy reading."[31] The practice has four stages that move from simple reading to a deeper consciousness of God. Since it begins and ends with the Bible, *Lectio Divina* is a good starting point for Christians who want to learn to meditate but are worried about influences from outside the faith.

HOW TO PRACTICE LECTIO DIVINA:

1. READ: The first stage is simply to read Scripture. Pick a short passage and read it slowly and carefully, repeating it until you're focused and calmly engaged with it.

2. REFLECT: The second stage is to reflect on the passage, thinking about it and what God is saying to you through it. This is the *hagah* or murmuring stage. Give it your full attention in mind, body, and

---

[31] http://ocarm.org/en/content/lectio/what-lectio-divina

spirit. Look at the passage from every angle. Another word for this stage is to "ruminate," which has the double meaning of deep thought and also cows chewing, swallowing, spitting up, and chewing again the same grass all day. Turning the passage over and over in our hearts and minds, like cows digest grass, is a good image for stage 2.

3. RESPOND: After reflecting on the passage with your mind, quiet your thinking and let your heart speak to God. Breathe and feel the inner message of the text back toward the God who inspired it and created you.

4. REST: Now let go of your feelings too. Rest in the Word of God for a while and listen to him in the depths of your soul. This rest, where you're no longer doing anything, is where God works and where spiritual transformation begins.

It might help you to keep a private journal of your experiences with meditation. Writing it down will help you process your insights and give you a moment to reflect on what to do with them in the outer reality of your life.

MEDITATING ON SCRIPTURE II: IMAGINATIVE PRAYER

Imaginative Prayer was developed by Ignatius of Loyola as an exercise to move the whole soul of the reader into the world of the text. His basic method engages the mind, the emotions, and the imagination, and although many of us already read like this, it can help to know what we're doing so that we can do it fully and intentionally. The core principle is to imagine yourself in a Bible story and to respond to its challenges and invitations. Imaginative Prayer is easier the more you know about the Bible and its background. If you need help understanding a passage, find a Bible scholar who can answer all your questions, and take notes on your conversation to use later.[32] Also use discernment and stick to passages where characters had a meaningful experience of God. Imagining yourself in one of the Bible's many stories of sexual assault or violent revenge will distract you at best, and at worst will work against the transformative process of becoming like Christ.

HOW TO PRACTICE IMAGINATIVE PRAYER:

1. READ: Read an appropriate story of an interaction between a human character and God, or especially Jesus in the gospels. It can also help to study the context to better imagine the scene.

2. IMAGINE: Quietly and prayerfully imagine the story again, this time with yourself as a witness or as the human character who encounters God. Try to imagine the entire scene with all 5 senses, and allow yourself to be drawn into the world of the text. If you have a hard time immersing yourself, you might imagine that you're a movie director considering how to film each moment in the scene. The goal is emotional resonance between yourself and the characters.

3. REACT: When the story reaches its critical moment, stop and react personally to the crisis. For example, in John 1:38 Jesus turns around, confronts two of John the Baptist's disciples who are

---

[32] You don't have to tell them what you're doing. Most knowledgeable people like to talk about their area of expertise just for the sake of it, and will be thrilled that you're interested whether or not they understand why.

following him at a distance, and says "What do you want?" If you're imagining yourself as one of the disciples, stop and prayerfully consider your own answer to Jesus' question. Pray your answer to him, telling him what you want and why you're following him. This can be a profoundly revealing moment of praise, confession, petition, or thanks, so take your time.

4. RESPOND: Let the scene play out to the end. Take note of how your thoughts, feelings, and awareness of God have changed.

Imaginative Prayer can be strange for adults who are used to television, movies, and video games doing all of our imagining for us. But there is good evidence that many of the biblical authors intentionally wrote in a way that draws their readers into the story to share in their own experiences of God.[33] We're not just invited to know what happened to the people of the Bible – through the biblical text, we're invited to let it happen to us, too.

PRACTICE 3: SILENT MEDITATION

Silent meditation is the practice of silence in both the outer and the inner reality. It's almost impossible for most of us to remove ourselves from the bustle and flow of a terribly busy world and sit in perfect silence. When we do, our mind continues to race, filling every quiet second with to-do lists and worries, or we're so tired and stressed that we fall asleep the moment we relax. Silent meditation is the long process of learning how to quiet our bodies, minds and spirits, and to sit in full awareness of the presence of God. This

---

[33] http://hts.org.za/index.php/HTS/article/view/1286

requires consistent, dedicated practice, recognition of the circumstances of your life that make it difficult, and a good sense of humor about yourself when you fail.

Silent meditation is the daily, practical embodiment of the spirit of prayerfulness taught and practiced by Christ himself. For Christians, the state of silent meditation is a restful state of disengagement from our guilt, worry, thoughts, judgments, pride, and self-image. It's an intentional practice of following Christ in his "pouring out" or self-emptying, as Paul teaches us to do.[34] Christ gave up his divinity, his dignity, his desire, his strength, his self-concern, and his own life. We do this in miniature as a daily meditation routine, entrusting our souls to God who will raise us in Christ's image just as he raised Christ himself.[35] Simply stated, in silent meditation we die to ourselves in prayer and wait patiently for God's Spirit to resurrect us to new life.

Recently, silent meditation in all religious traditions has been the subject of an extensive study overseen by neurologist Dr. Andrew Newberg.[36] According to his research, silent meditation offers amazing benefits for cognitive, emotional, and physical health, visible in most beginners after only 8 weeks of practice for 15 minutes a day. If you're skeptical about meditation from a religious perspective, Dr. Newberg's work from the medical perspective is worth considering.

---

[34] Philippians 2:5-11.
[35] Romans 8:11.
[36] Andrew B. Newberg and Mark Waldman, *How God Changes Your Brain: Breakthrough Findings From A Leading Neurologist,* Ballantine Books, 2009.

SILENT MEDITATION I: CENTERING PRAYER

Centering Prayer as a formal method was developed fairly recently by Thomas Keating, but probably has its roots in ancient Christian tradition. In Centering Prayer, a sacred word or phrase is chosen to "center" the mind and free it from distractions. The goal is to disengage from the constant stream of passing, anxious thoughts that our minds generate so that we can find rest in the simple, quiet presence of God. It's not an effort to suppress or silence our thoughts, since that would be engaging with them in a negative way. Instead, it's the practice of letting them go and returning gently to the center and the sacred word. Deep peace is the indication that God has brought you to your center, and is a cause for thankfulness.

HOW TO PRACTICE CENTERING PRAYER:

1. CHOOSE A WORD.

Select a sacred word or short phrase that represents your openness to God's presence and work in you. "Love," "presence," "Christ," or simply "You" are examples of words that might work well. "Here I am" or "Be still" might be good phrases. Pick something that has personal meaning for you. You can try out different words for the first several days until you find one that fits you well, but try not to switch words in the middle of prayer. Wait until the next day to try a new word.

2. INTRODUCE THE WORD.

Sit still with your eyes closed and introduce your word to your mind and to God. Hold your attention on it as long as you can, and remember to breathe.

3. RETURN TO CENTER.

After a few moments you'll notice your mind drift away from this new "center." Let your thoughts go and gently bring your attention back to your word. Don't get frustrated with yourself for getting distracted. You've grown up in a busy, distracted world and it's not your fault that your attention has been trained to wander. Don't judge yourself or the effectiveness of your prayer. There's no way to win or lose at meditation. Your goal is silence, not victory or achievement, and there's no trophy in the world for the most silent meditator.

4. SILENCE.

When your prayer is over, sit in silence for a few moments. Don't be in a hurry to return to the bustle of the day. Enjoy the calm and loving presence of God. When you do get up and leave, don't think too much about "how it went," "what happened," or if you were "successful." Let it be what it was, live your life, and do it again tomorrow. Persistence and humility must rule silent meditation, and nothing kills the spirit of prayerfulness faster than an analytical mind expecting results. In this one area of your life, give yourself permission to stop worrying about being the best.

Here are some optional but recommended practices for Centering Prayer:

1. It's a good idea to set a timer. No one has unlimited time to pray, and knowing that your timer will tell you when it's over will help you postpone your worry about the rest of the day

38

until after you've finished praying.

2. Start small. When you begin, try to stay centered for 5 minutes and work up to 15 over the course of a week or two. Prayer, and especially silent meditation, takes practice.

3. It can be helpful to read a short passage of Scripture before and after you practice Centering Prayer. The last thing you before you close your eyes, and the first thing you see after you open them, will be the Word of God. That will set the tone for your prayer time, and for the rest of the day as you get up and move on to other things.[37]

SILENT MEDITATION II: ABIDE/DIE/REST

The next level of silent meditation is practiced by many different spiritual traditions and has many names such as Contemplation, Listening Prayer, and Mindfulness. In Christian practice it's best described by Jesus' teaching to "abide in me, and I in you,"[38] by his instruction to "lose your life for my sake,"[39] and by the concept in Hebrews of "entering God's rest."[40] Abiding in Christ, dying to yourself, and entering God's rest is complete non-action and letting go, the total abandonment of your desires, projects, judgments, self-defenses, and narratives. Think of this kind of prayer as a daily protest against the world's demands for productivity, position, and justifying yourself. When you sit in silent surrender, thinking

---

[37] Contemplative Outreach offers a free Centering Prayer app for smartphones that includes a meditation timer and allows you to select Bible passages and prayers to start and end your session (see the Appendix 2: Resources & Further Reading).

[38] John 15:4.

[39] Matthew 10:39.

[40] Hebrews 4:10-13.

nothing, doing nothing other than loving God and being loved by God, you'll experience the spirit of prayerfulness and share in the life of God as Christ did.

HOW TO PRACTICE ABIDING PRAYER:

1. **SIT QUIETLY.** There is nothing to do, so don't.

2. **BETRAY YOUR EGO.** Reject your mind's offer to make you the star of the show, to analyze how it's going, or to criticize your experience. Just be another thing that God has made, in love and peace with all the other things that he has made.

3. **LET YOUR THOUGHTS GO.** Stop thinking. Sit and breathe. Everything – everything! – else can wait.

4. **RECEIVE.** God made you, you exist, and he loves you. Christ saved you and you're a child of God. The Spirit dwells with you and transforms you with or without your help. That is enough.

5. **FORGIVE.** Let yourself be what you are, and let everything else be what it is. When your meditation is over, walk through the rest of your day without needing to be the protagonist in the story of the world around you. Honor every other creature as they are, without letting them change what you are. Ask God to open your eyes to see his light in all things.

This practice can have a profound impact on your spirituality, but it will take dedication and practice to maintain an abiding or restful mind. Stick with it, you'll be happy that you did.

CHAPTER 3: PRAYING WITH PRAYER BEADS

Any of the prayers in this section can be prayed with or without beads. No matter how you pray it, some form of the Full Circle prayer given below should find its way into your daily practice. Prayer beads do have their benefits, however, if you can learn to get comfortable with them. Try them out if you can.

HISTORY

Some ancient Christian prayer communities used stones to count their prayers. A person would sit at a table or on the ground with a pile of small stones in front of them. After each prayer, they would remove one stone from the pile and place it in a new pile until all the stones had been moved.

A handful of rocks isn't always available, and some Christians began to carry their prayer stones with them in small pouches. Even in a pouch, stones are easy to lose or drop, so a set of beads strung together on a loop was developed. A string of beads was simple to transport, harder to lose, and the beads only had to be counted once when the set was made.

Prayer beads have been popular in many religious communities and used in different ways throughout history. In Western Christianity today they have a strong association with Roman Catholic prayers to the Virgin Mary, but Christian prayer beads existed centuries before they were used for Marian prayers like the Rosary. A very common Eastern variation on prayer beads is the *komboskini* or *chotki* used by Greek and Russian Orthodox Christians, who use a series of special knots tied in a loop of rope instead of beads.

WHY BEADS?

Besides the history, why count prayers at all? How can a string of beads help us maintain a spirit of prayerfulness? Here are four reasons for including beads in your prayer practice:

1. TO FOCUS YOUR ATTENTION.

Learning to sit still and quiet your mind can be very frustrating, especially at first. Praying with beads or stones gives your hands something to do while you pray in mind and heart. This involves your body in your prayer practice, helping you to bring your whole self into awareness of God's presence. As with any of our practices, if we think of beads as a tool to move God we've already crossed into idolatry. If you're humble and honest about beads being a tool to bring your wandering mind into harmony with your fidgeting body, prayer beads can be an aid to developing the spirit of prayerfulness.

2. TO STRUCTURE YOUR PRAYERS.

Structure can give you a reliable pattern of prayer that you can use easily when you're especially distracted, tired, or anxious. It takes less effort to pray consistently when you have a familiar method that's easy to remember. Without structure to your prayers, it's easy to get distracted and jump from thought to thought. You might even begin with prayer and end up thinking about other concerns. Adding structure to your prayer time keeps your mind on task and helps you to be sincere in what you're doing.

3. TO EXERCISE YOUR IMAGINATION.

A common use for prayer beads is to count the repetition of the same prayer over and over again, which isn't very creative. However, beads can also be used to exercise your mind and imagination while you pray. In the "Full Circle" prayer listed below, we praise God in seven ways, confess seven sins, pray for seven concerns, and thank God for seven blessings. Most of us can quickly think of two or three things to say in each category, but working to think of seven unique things forces us to stretch our spirits and imaginations.

4. AS A TIMER FOR MEDITATION.

A timer can be a great help with meditation practices such as Centering Prayer, Abiding/Contemplative Prayer, and Listening

Prayer. Having a timer will push you to stay in full concentration and openness to God until your meditation is over. A timer will also help you relax as you meditate. Knowing that your prayer time will end after several minutes helps to postpone the pressure of a busy schedule until after you have finished your meditation. But if your only timer is a smartphone or smartwatch app, your meditation and your concentration will be constantly interrupted by notifications. Beads can replace electronic timers for most meditation practices, and unless they break while you're praying, they won't interrupt your prayer flow.

WHICH BEADS?

Here are a few things to consider when making your own prayer beads. First, beads aren't jewelry. They're for prayer, not display, and shouldn't be designed to draw the attention of others to your prayer life. Remember, the spirit of prayerfulness is private and your beads need to reflect that. Second, beads are supposed to help you pray continually. They should be small enough to easily carry with you and strong enough to survive in your pocket or purse. Consider the durability of your beads, especially when choosing the string or wire. And third, some Christians may be uncomfortable using a cross as an emblem. You can finish the end of your beads however you choose, but keep in mind that Christian bead prayers are still prayers through Jesus Christ. Choose an emblem that will help you remember the God you're praying to, and in whose name you're praying.

DIAGRAM OF A BASIC SET OF PRAYER BEADS

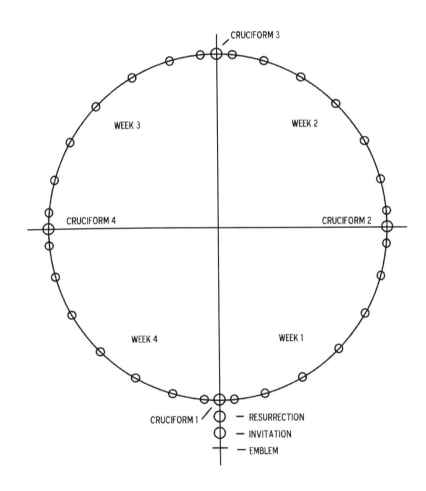

PRACTICE 4: PRAYERS FOR BEADS

Three easy-to-learn methods for using standard prayer beads are given below. Of course, there are too many other ways to pray with beads to list them all here. If you want to expand your practice or need tips on making prayer beads, *A Bead And A Prayer: A Beginner's Guide To Protestant Prayer Beads* by Kristen E. Vincent is the resource I've found most helpful and the source I've used for this chapter.

BEAD PRAYER I: FULL CIRCLE PRAYER[41]

This simple bead prayer combines and balances the major Christian prayer forms: worship, confession, petition, and thanks. It's a great way for busy people to train themselves to pray at all times, and for anxious people to develop their prayer relationship with God beyond simply asking for what we need. Carry your beads with you and pray the Full Circle throughout the day as often as you can, and in response to whatever situation you face.

HOW TO PRAY A FULL CIRCLE WITH BEADS:

1. **START WITH THE EMBLEM OF THE CROSS.** In the spirit of prayerfulness address God through Christ, who died for your sins and calls you into new life through his resurrection.

2. **MOVE TO THE INVITATION.** Ask God to fill you with the Holy Spirit and to work in your soul wherever and however the Spirit chooses.

3. **MOVE TO THE RESURRECTION.** Put your hope in the God who raised

---

[41] From Kristen E. Vincent, *A Bead And A Prayer: A Beginner's Guide To Protestant Prayer Beads* (Upper Room, 2013).

Jesus from the dead. Trust that he can make you into a new creature too, right now.

4. MOVE TO CRUCIFORM 1. Address God with a heart of praise. Pray 7 praises to God as you move from bead to bead in Week 1.

Praises can be things God has done in creation or in your life, or things that he has promised to do in the future. They can also be amazing things about God's power or character. If you need inspiration, reading the Psalms will teach you how to be creative and sincere in your praises to God.

5. MOVE TO CRUCIFORM 2. Address God with a heart of humility and repentance. As you move through the beads of Week 2, confess 7 sins, failures, or weaknesses to God. For each one, ask for God's forgiveness through the cross of Christ, and ask for help and healing through the work of the Holy Spirit.

Repentance comes from the Holy Spirit. True repentance means crucifying your pride, being honest with God about what you're not, and openly receiving the conviction and discipline of the Spirit. It also means humbly asking for God's forgiveness and his help to better honor him with your thoughts and actions. Most importantly, it opens you to the hope that, despite your failures, God really can work in your life and transform you into Christ's image. True repentance isn't the same as self-condemnation. Self-condemnation is a constant, guilty remembering of all that you've done to offend God until you become convinced that you're unworthy of God's acceptance, forgiveness, and love. Self-condemnation comes from evil because it blinds you to Christ's saving work on the cross and removes the hope of Christ's invitation to share the life of God.

6. MOVE TO CRUCIFORM 3. Address God with the heart of a child, and trust your Father to provide for your needs. Move from bead to bead in Week 3 and commit 7 worries or needs to the care of God.

Jesus says to "ask for whatever you wish in my name, and it will be done for you."[42] Peter teaches to "cast all your cares on God, for he cares for you."[43] But Jesus also teaches us to pray simply for "our daily bread,"[44] and James warns us against asking for things with selfish motives or desires.[45] Prayer as petition isn't a method to move God to get you what you want. Instead, prayer is an act of faith that God "knows what you need before you ask it"[46] and will "give good gifts to his children"[47] as he sees fit. Praying for worries and needs in humility is a way to humble yourself, admit your inability to change your own circumstances, and entrust your whole self to the care of God.[48] It's incredibly freeing to be the one who trusts, and to let God do the worrying.

7. MOVE TO CRUCIFORM 4. Address God with a heart of thankfulness. Moving from bead to bead in Week 4, remember 7 ways that God has blessed you. Thank him for his loving presence in your life.

We often feel far from God because we can't feel his presence or see his action in the worries of our present crisis. When we stop to

---

[42] John 15:7.
[43] 1 Peter 5:7
[44] Matthew 6:11.
[45] James 4.
[46] Matthew 6:8.
[47] Matthew 7:11.
[48] 1 Peter 4:19.

thank God for what he has already done for us, we become receptive to his presence in the daily answers to prayer that he always provides. Thankfulness also puts our present worries into perspective. It compares our current struggles with the lifetime of blessing that has come before them, and gives us hope that the God who has blessed us in the past will bless us again.

8. MOVE BACK THROUGH CRUCIFORM 1, RESURRECTION, INVITATION, AND OUT TO THE CROSS. On Cruciform 1, thank God for hearing your prayers. On Resurrection, thank God for the hope of new life in Christ. On Invitation, thank God for the presence and work of the Holy Spirit in your soul. At the Cross, thank God for his forgiveness. Ask him for help to carry your own cross and to live like Christ throughout the rest of your day.

BEAD PRAYER II: LISTENING PRAYER

Listening Prayer trains us to be at peace in the presence of God. It silences the constant chatter of our minds and hearts and opens us to the possibility that God might want to speak to us. Listening Prayer is very difficult at first because most people associate prayer with busily asking God for things. Others want to hear God's audible voice with clear instructions and don't know how to wait for the "still, small voice"[49] of the Spirit. But it does get easier with practice, so be gracious to yourself as you learn to be still.

HOW TO PRAY A LISTENING PRAYER WITH BEADS:

Listening Prayer requires focus and peace, so find a place where

[49] 1 Kings 19:12.

you won't be interrupted for a few minutes.

1. Move through the Cross, the Invitation, and the Resurrection following steps 1-3 of the "Full Circle" prayer above.

2. On Cruciform 1, repeat a short verse or phrase that expresses your intention to listen to the voice of God. A few biblical examples are:

- Samuel 3:10 - "Speak Lord, for your servant is listening"
- Psalm 46:10 – "Be still and know that I am God"
- Luke 1:38 – "I am the Lord's servant"

3. Move slowly and silently from bead to bead in Week 1, breathing deeply. Quiet your mind and listen to the silence. Wait in expectation for God to speak, but don't be desperate for "something to happen." If you really are listening for God to speak to you, you'll have to learn to trust that he will, whenever and however he chooses.

In Ephesians 1, Paul's prayer for his church isn't that God will send them a new or special message, but that the "eyes of their hearts" would be opened to comprehend what God is doing and what he has already done. This voice of God is present in all things at all times, and is especially clear in Jesus Christ. Paul teaches that in God the whole creation "lives and moves and has our being."[50] In Romans, he writes that "from him and through him and to him are all things."[51] To the Corinthian church he writes "For it is the God who said, 'Let light shine out of darkness,' who has shone in our hearts to give the light of the knowledge of the glory of God in the face of Jesus Christ."[52] As much as you might desire a personal message

---

[50] Acts 17:28.
[51] Romans 11:36.

from God to you, most Listening Prayer is about becoming sensitive and aware of what God's voice is already and always speaking in everything that he has made. Ask God to open the eyes and ears of your heart to see his work and hear his voice in all of creation, and to understand his full communication through the cross and resurrection of Jesus.

4. At Cruciform 2, 3, and 4 repeat your verse or phrase. Continue breathing deeply and listening in silence from bead to bead through Weeks 2, 3 and 4.

5. When you get back around to Cruciform 1, you can either pray around the loop again or exit back through the Resurrection, the Invitation, and the Cross. At the Resurrection, ask for help hearing God's voice in the hope of a renewed creation. At the Invitation, ask for help hearing the Holy Spirit speaking through all of your experiences in life. At the Cross ask for help hearing God in the incarnation, teachings, work, suffering, death, burial, resurrection, and return of Christ, and for help understanding how carrying your cross can change the shape of your life.

BEAD PRAYER III: BEADS AS A MEDITATION TIMER

If you need to time your meditation but want to be fully disconnected from technology while you meditate, beads can help. In Centering Prayer, each bead can represent one repetition of your sacred word. At each bead, breathe in and out, focus your attention on your word, and move on to the next bead. Repeat for a desired

---

[52] 2 Corinthians 4:6.

number of passes around the loop. In Abiding Prayer, the mind isn't actively repeating a sacred word or phrase, but simply and subconsciously resting in God. For this practice you can breathe slowly and deeply at each bead for a desired number of passes around the loop while you die to yourself and rest in God's presence.

CHAPTER 4: BREATH PRAYERS AND MINDFUL CHORES

PRACTICE 5: BREATH PRAYERS

Breath prayers are short prayers that can be prayed in a single in/out breath. They are a simple way to pray "in the Spirit and at all times and on every occasion." After a morning practice of reading and meditation, we often rush back into our busy lives and struggle to hold onto our awareness of God's presence. Having a breath prayer ready to pray whenever you feel stressed will ground you and help you maintain a spirit of prayerfulness throughout the day. If you can breathe, you can pray a breath prayer.

Just like breathing, a typical Breath Prayer has an inhalation and an exhalation. On the inhalation we address God, and on the exhalation we engage with God. The classic Jesus Prayer both addresses God and engages with him, and can be prayed in a single breath:

Inhaling, we pray: "Lord Jesus Christ, Son of God…"
and exhaling we pray: "…have mercy on me, a sinner."

Remember, creativity in prayer doesn't require special vocabulary or language skills. The art of prayer comes from the depth of meaning and strength of soul that we give to our simple words. Like the Lord's Prayer, a Breath Prayer is nothing fancy, but in a spirit of prayerfulness a persistently repeated Breath Prayer can be a powerful way to engage the presence of God.

HOW TO PRAY A BREATH PRAYER:

1. Think about how to address God with your inward breath. Think of his names, titles, and actions in Scripture and choose something that is meaningful to you.

2. Think about how to engage God with your outward breath. This step is usually a spiritual request, such as "have mercy on me, a sinner," although it doesn't have to be. Prayers for wisdom, guidance, help, protection, and forgiveness all work well. Or you can ask the Spirit to teach you specific spiritual attitudes or to better embody the image of Christ.

3. Put the two halves together, and practice your Breath Prayer a few times with big in/out breaths to get the rhythm. Concentrate on praying it with your whole being.

4. When you feel pressured throughout the day or just want to return to the spirit of prayerfulness, take a deep breath and

pray your Breath Prayer. If you kept count, it wouldn't be at all surprising to find that you'd prayed over a hundred times throughout the day - no small improvement for those of us who struggle to find the time to pray once! The secret is all in your breath.

PRACTICE 6: MINDFUL CHORES

Mindfulness and Mindful Chores aren't necessarily classic Christian practices, but the basic concept can be found throughout the New Testament. To slaves and household workers Paul writes, "Whatever you do, do it whole-heartedly for the Lord and not for men, knowing that from the Lord you will receive your inheritance as your reward."[53] In our time most of us do our own housework, and most of the jobs we do outside the home include dull, repetitive elements. Paul's challenge is to approach even tedious and disagreeable work with a spirit of prayerfulness and a sense of God's presence. Our busy lives are structured in such a way that if we save our spirituality for our free time, we'll only allow ourselves to be aware of God in a tiny fraction of our day. But if we open ourselves to God in the mundane and ordinary work of life, we can truly learn the fullness of what Paul meant when he said "in him we live and move and have our being."

HOW TO PRACTICE MINDFUL CHORES:

1. APPROACH YOUR WORK WITH SPIRITUAL INTENT.

Take a moment to pray for an awareness of God's presence in the

---

[53] Colossians 3:23.

boring and the tedious. Decide before you start that you're going to do whatever you do for the Lord. Ask the Spirit to teach you about your relationship with God and creation through the task, and stay receptive to his still, small voice. It can help to have a Breath Prayer that includes this request ready to pray throughout your work.

2. BE FULLY PRESENT AND OPEN TO THE TASK AT HAND.

While we do chores, most of us are thinking about what we'd rather be doing or what we're going to do when we finish. Listening to music or watching videos while you work can make the time go faster, but to practice Mindful Chores you'll need to eliminate anything that will dull your awareness of the moment. Keep your mind, body, and spirit present and focused together on what you're doing. Be sincere about what parts of the task are enjoyable and what parts aren't. Pray your Breath Prayer as you work, and pay attention to the deep lessons in the cycles of ordinary activities.

3. BE THANKFUL FOR THE REASONS THAT MAKE THE WORK NECESSARY.

When you have to wash dishes, you were first blessed with something to eat. When you have to change diapers, you were first blessed with children. When you have to do housework, you were first blessed with a place to live. When you have tedious work to complete at the office, you were first blessed with a job and the skills to provide for yourself and your family. Most of us prayed for all of these blessings before we received them, and God answered our prayers. The practice of Mindful Chores is doing the work that comes with God's blessings in a spirit of thankfulness. Proverbs says "You can keep your barn clean if you don't have any oxen, but you need the strength of the ox to produce a good harvest."[54] Thankfulness means gratitude for the ox and the mess that comes with it, because the mess makes the harvest possible.

4. BE HUMBLE ENOUGH TO COMPLETE THE TASK WELL.

Humility is the key to Mindful Chores. If you don't do the tedious work, someone else will have to. Put others first and do it yourself. Sacrifice the time and effort you could be spending on doing something personally satisfying and carry some of the small burdens of the people you love. Doing it for their praise or so that they'll owe you, even emotionally, isn't humility. Making a show of your great sacrifice with your comments or body language isn't the private attitude of the spirit of prayerfulness, and there will be no spiritual reward. Doing a favor for someone in a way that interrupts what they're doing to draw attention to yourself, or leaves a mess that they'll have to clean up, is no favor. Proverbs says that "Blessing your neighbor loudly in the early morning will be taken as a curse."[55] A blessing that's all about you is no blessing at all. We also lose the spirit of prayerfulness when we do our daily work in competition with others. Take your time to work as well as you can, then be happy with your effort. The practice of Mindful Chores has no room for comparison, self-criticism, or self-promotion. Be humble enough to work happily, for no recognition, for no repayment, and in consideration of the needs of others. Be humble enough to see your task through to the end, and clean up after yourself when you're

---

[54] Proverbs 14:4.
[55] Proverbs 27:14.

done.

5. LEAVE YOUR WORK WITH OPENNESS TO THE NEXT TASK.

The cycles of housework, childcare, and business never end. Sometimes it seems like we spend a lot of effort on meaningless things and never see progress – the dishes always get dirty again. Of course, an unbroken cycle of work is the sign of an unbroken cycle of God's blessing. But best of all, if we're receptive to the Spirit and see the tedious, ordinary tasks of regular life as an opportunity to be transformed into Christ's image, we understand that real, eternal movement in our souls can happen through the repetition of our daily chores. The progress is in *you*. When you finish each task, be thankful for completing it and move on to the next thing. Even washing the same dishes over and over for a lifetime can transform you into Christ's image, if you wash them mindfully and in a spirit of prayerfulness.

CHAPTER 5: PRAYING THE HOURS, PRAYER BOOKS, AND THE LITURGICAL CALENDAR

PRAYER ON A SCHEDULE

The Christian custom of praying at set times of the day has its roots in ancient Jewish tradition. The Psalms speak of the typical prayer times as morning, noon, evening, and midnight. While a captive of the Persian Empire, the prophet Daniel "had windows in his upper chamber open toward Jerusalem… he kneeled three times a day and prayed and gave thanks before his God, as he always did."[56] It seems that the early Christians continued the Jewish tradition and

---

[56] Daniel 6:10.

prayed at regular hours throughout the day – the third hour (morning), the sixth hour (noon), the ninth hour (evening), and midnight.[57] Jesus' own prayer practice involved praying very early in the morning, giving thanks for meals throughout the day, and sometimes spending all night alone in prayer.[58]

PRACTICE 7: THE HOURS

The discipline of praying at regular times throughout the day has obvious benefits for maintaining a spirit of prayerfulness. Scripture reading and prayer time in the early morning aligns your spirit before your day really begins, helping you to continue in an awareness of the presence of God through whatever else happens. In the evening, dedicated prayer time helps you review the day and commit your cares and worries to God before you rest, which will help you sleep much better. Ignore your daily prayer practice, and you leave yourself open for a spirit of anxiety and loneliness to dominate your life. If you don't make prayer a habit and schedule time for it each day, you'll always be at the mercy of your emotions or the pace of a busy world. You'll tend to chase deep experiences of God when you're desperate, when you "feel like it," or when you "have time," but then you'll grind along in frustration in the long valleys between spiritual peaks. Remember, persistence is a crucial element of the spirit of prayerfulness. Patiently show up every day to open your spirit to the Spirit of God, and you'll see God work stable, durable results in personal growth and the development of Christ-

---

[57] Acts 2:15, 3:1, 10:3, 10: 9, 10:31, 16:25.
[58] Mark 1:35; Matthew 14:19-21; Luke 6:12.

like character.

HOW TO PRAY THE HOURS:

1. COMMIT.

Commit to one week of daily prayers at a set time. You can make adjustments to your prayer schedule after a week, but the experience of fighting through the obligations of life to stick to your schedule will show you what it takes to be consistent.

2. FIND YOUR RHYTHM.

Pick a place in the rhythm of the day's activities when you'll be able to find some peace and quiet. Early morning before everyone else wakes up has always been a popular prayer time, and so has the evening after the day's work is over and the children are asleep. In ancient cultures the middle of the night was understood as an especially sacred time, called the "quiet hour," while for many in our time the only quiet hour we get is our lunch break in the middle of a shift. All of our lives are hectic, demanding, and different, so pick a time that works for you and make it a daily sanctuary for seeking an awareness of God.

3. PLAN AHEAD.

It can help to have a plan or a routine so that you won't spend what little prayer time you have wondering what to read in Scripture or how you're going to pray. Decide on a Bible reading plan or a spiritual exercise beforehand, and go into your prayer time prepared. Don't be afraid of familiar routines - a regular hour of prayer might be the only stable, reliable moment in your whole day.

4. ASK FOR HELP.

If you're a parent of small children or someone with a demanding job, you may need the help of others to find a moment of peace. Ask your spouse to watch the kids for 20 minutes or ask a coworker to answer the phone, then go somewhere to pray. Having a plan and sticking to it for a set amount of time will help you feel like you're not abusing the help of others.

5. MAKE SACRIFICES.

You may need to sacrifice a few minutes of your leisure time to seek the presence of God. Many of us believe that we don't have a spare 20 minutes for prayer in our whole day, and yet somehow find the time to binge watch whole seasons of TV shows before bed. It shouldn't come as a surprise that *spiritual discipline might actually require some disciple or self-control.* And it's also about priorities. Do you really want to live in a fuller awareness of God's presence in your life? "Where your treasure is, there your heart will be also."[59]

PRACTICE 8: PRAYER BOOKS AND THE LITURGICAL CALENDAR

Today, many Jewish and Christian traditions continue the custom of daily hours of prayer. Some use specific Psalms and Bible passages for each hour. Others include historical prayers that aren't found in Scripture. Many faith communities publish prayer books for daily use, with prayers and Bible readings laid out for each day of a weekly cycle. These are often linked to the yearly "Liturgical Calendar," an ancient calendar that's meant to orient the church to

---

[59] Matt. 6:21

the seasons and holidays representing the major events of the life of Christ, like Christmas and Easter. These prayer books can be simple and easy to use, such as *Celtic Prayers from Iona: The Heart of Celtic Spirituality* by J.P. Newell, or incredibly detailed and difficult to follow, such as the Catholic *Roman Breviary* or the Anglican *Book of Common Prayer.* Some prayer books, like Walter Brueggemann's *Prayers for a Privileged People,* don't mention the hours at all, and are only loosely tied to the church calendar. They represent devotional prayers written by a spiritual teacher organized around a specific theme.

Praying the Psalms or using a book of written prayers can have several benefits. The Psalms are especially helpful for giving you permission to be bold in the heart and language of your prayers. David and the other psalmists regularly prayed things that most of us wouldn't be brave enough to say to God ourselves. By following their example you can go places with God that you might normally be afraid to. A well-written prayer book by a wise spiritual teacher can also open your spirit to a new awareness of God that you might not have encountered on your own. Or it can force you to confront personal, spiritual issues that you would rather ignore. An organized prayer book can help you develop persistence, since even on the days when you're not "feeling it," you'll always have something to pray. And a prayer book that engages the Liturgical Calendar can help align your spirit with the seasons of the church, preparing you months in advance for a deeper experience of holidays like Christmas and Easter along with the wider Christian community.

CHAPTER 6: LAMENT AND FASTING

Suffering is the common experience of all human life. While some suffer more than others during our lifetimes, all of us pass through the uncontrollable, unbeatable suffering of dying and death. Some Christians have the attitude that we can transcend suffering through faith and positive thinking, but this isn't a true or biblical understanding of the human experience at all. Suffering that can be ignored with positive thinking isn't real suffering. Many of the people who wrote the Bible knew real suffering with an intimacy that only a few in our time and culture can match, and they never denied the reality of their pain. The writers of Scripture dealt with their suffering not by hiding it or quietly enduring it, but by crying their pain and abandonment clearly, loudly, and spiritually to God.

The spiritual expression of grief, sorrow, and anguish is called Lament.

PRACTICE 9: LAMENT

There is a lot more Lament in the Bible than most people realize. There are around 50 community and individual songs of Lament in the Psalms, which is about one third of the *entire book*. The prophets such as Isaiah and Ezekiel include major sections of Lament in their work, and some books like Habakkuk and Job are almost completely devoted to Lament. There are expressions of Lament in the New Testament, such as Jesus' tears over Jerusalem[60] and Paul's comment that "all of creation is groaning for the sons of God to be revealed," waiting for the whole universe to be made new.[61] And of course Lamentations is an entire Old Testament book with Lament as its title.

The God revealed in the Bible clearly allows plenty of doubt, protest, and mourning in the spiritual lives of his people as we face the suffering and disorientation of a difficult world. Instead of punishing us for our lack of faith, God actually invites us to share our experiences of deep pain with him. Crying out in sorrow or even outrage can be a profound spiritual experience that opens us to God's healing presence. If our goal is to pray with true sincerity and in all circumstances, sometimes Lament is the only real option.

The prayers of Lament in Scripture express frustrations and despair, but they don't stay there. Biblical Lament tends to follow a

---

[60] Matthew 23:37-39.
[61] Romans 8:19.

pattern of movement from hopelessness to hope. This process is never rushed, and often the frustration of the writer isn't fully resolved, even by hope. When hope is nothing more than a few grim words at the end, or when hope isn't given the last word, hopelessness and hope are allowed to live in a dynamic tension that accurately reflects the hard reality of human life. But in biblical Laments, a small spark of hope almost always exists, and receiving that spark in our worst moments is a gift that can only come from an encounter with the living God.

Hope in suffering is the Spirit of Jesus, who "for the joy set before him endured the cross, despising the shame."[62] The painful process of suffering, death, and resurrection is what God uses to bring new life to his creatures. In our spiritual development and in our whole experience of life, we suffer and die as Christ did. Like Christ, our only hope is that God will raise us out of our suffering and death to new life. Prayer, and often Lament, is what we do in the time between, as we wait for the Spirit of God to work and make all things new.

Lament in the spirit of prayerfulness requires intense sincerity about your suffering or the suffering of others. Sometimes it might feel like your boldness comes at the expense of your humility, since on a basic level Lament challenges the reality that God has allowed. As you're learning, it can be helpful to pray through the Psalms of Lament.[63] With great language skill, the Psalmists walk an

---

[62] Hebrews 12:2.
[63] See Appendix 1: The Psalms By Type.

incredibly fine line between serious protest directed at God and open rebellion against God's sovereignty. That line is where good Lament lives. The selections from the Psalms of Lament given below will serve as examples to help you either pray the Psalms themselves or respond in your own words to the struggles of your life.

HOW TO PRACTICE LAMENT PRAYER:

1. OWN YOUR PAIN. FIND ITS SOURCE. AND IDENTIFY ITS EFFECTS IN YOU.

Sickness, betrayal, the success of an enemy, political injustice, the grief of losing a loved one, personal sin and addiction, a sense of God's abandonment – there are far too many causes of human suffering to list here. The first step in praying a Lament is to acknowledge that you're suffering, and to be honest with yourself about the reasons. In all suffering there's an outside element and a personal element – what's happening that's causing your pain, and why is your soul responding to it with grief? Then ask yourself what your pain feels like, and pray it all to God.

Psalm 42:9-10, paraphrased:

I said to God, my rock,

"Why have you forgotten me?

Why do I have to walk around in mourning

because the enemy has power over me?

It feels like a fatal wound in my body

When my enemies taunt me,

Always saying,

'Where is your God?'"

2. UNDERSTAND WHY YOUR PAIN DOESN'T REPRESENT THE TRUTH YOU KNOW ABOUT GOD.

Suffering happens when what we need or expect in life is denied. We believe in a good God who cares for creation and is present to each of us. But sometimes reality gives us evidence that contradicts that belief. The next step in a Lament prayer is to pray your expectations of God and your disappointments to him.

Psalm 22:3-8, paraphrased:

"God, you're supposed to be Holy,

Your throne is our praise to you.

Our ancestors trusted in you, and you saved them.

They cried out to you and were saved,

You didn't let them be put to shame.

But me? I'm a worm and not a man;

They all scorn me, and everyone hates me.

Everyone who sees me mocks me,

Making faces and shaking their heads, saying,

"If you trust God so much, let him save you;

If God loves you so much, why doesn't he rescue you?"

3. CRY YOUR PAIN TO GOD AS BOLDLY AS YOU CAN.

The Psalms use a lot of exaggerated language that can sound barbaric to readers who are used to polite religion. But suffering isn't polite – it's cruel, unreasonable, and offensive, and there are times when our prayer language needs to match the ugliness of our situation.[64] The Psalms give us permission to creatively and boldly express the terrible realities of suffering in our cries to God.

Psalm 137 isn't an invitation to be morbid for its own sake, nor is it God's blessing on human violence. Sadly, it's a true expression of the spiritual torment experienced by the victims of a genocide. What other words could ever sincerely express their grief?

Psalm 137:8-9, paraphrased:

"O daughter Babylon, you destroyer!

The ones who pay you back for what you did to us will be blessed,

The ones who take your little ones and smash them against the rocks!"

4. PRESENT THE CHALLENGE OF YOUR OWN FAITHFULNESS TO GOD AND COMMIT TO WAITING FOR HIS HELP.

A startling dimension of the biblical prayers of Lament is the way many writers seem to challenge God with their continued faithfulness. They resolve to remain righteous, despite all the evidence that God has abandoned them. They hope that God will remember them, show them compassion, and change their circumstances. This might seem innocent on the surface, but in many cases it's actually a form of arguing with God. When you maintain your own guiltlessness in the face of suffering, you place the burden of righteousness on God, demanding that he take you seriously and move to align reality with your expectations of him.[65] Of course God isn't bound by your attitude of defiance, and can do whatever he wants.[66] But some of the Bible's most powerful moments between

---

[64] See Walter Brueggemann, *Praying the Psalms: Engaging Scripture and the Life of the Spirit,* Wipf and Stock Publishers, 2007.

[65] This is what Job does throughout the book…

God and people happen in the tension when God has been challenged to act righteously by a grieving, righteous person, or by an admitted sinner who demands mercy from a merciful God. Hope is often the simple, defiant expectation that God will fulfill his responsibilities as the Creator of the universe and as the Father of each of us, whether we deserve it or not.

Habakkuk 3:17-18, paraphrased:

Even though the fig tree doesn't blossom,

And the vines give no fruit,

The olive trees give no harvest,

And the fields don't grow crops,

Even though there's no sheep in the fold,

And no herd in the corral,

I will still rejoice in the Lord

And praise the God of my salvation.

5. WAIT.

Prayers of Lament from creatures to their Creator are just one side of suffering. Our hope as Christians is that God knows what we're going through and will respond. God in Christ walked the path of a human being, suffering severely to bring us the hope of the resurrection. He promised to always care for us, and that his Spirit would be with us no matter what we go through.[67] Laments aren't meant to be the final word on suffering. Their power is in their ability to open the conversation between our suffering souls and

---

[66] … and this is God's answer to Job's defiance at the end.

[67] John 14:18.

71

God. The final step in the practice of Lament is to bravely live in the tension that your prayer creates, always attentive and hopeful that God will speak when and how he chooses.

PRACTICE 10: FASTING

Fasting is abstaining from food or the fulfillment of some other need or desire for a period of time. Most spiritual traditions include some form of fasting, usually for one of two reasons – to establish ritual purity, or as a Lament in times of mourning or regret.

Fasting is mentioned in the Bible in both contexts. The first fast mentioned in Scripture is a community Lament after the tribe of Benjamin slaughtered the other tribes of Israel in battle during a terrible a civil war.[68] David fasted in regret over his own adulterous and homicidal actions, and to beg God for mercy for his infant son.[69] The Jews who returned to Israel from the Babylonian captivity fasted to purify themselves before the journey.[70] Jesus fasted for 40 days and nights to prepare himself for Satan's temptations.[71] The apostles prayed and fasted when they were seeking the leading of the Spirit on specific difficult issues.[72]

The curious thing about fasting in the Bible is that there are no clear reasons given for *why* we should fast in the first place. It simply exists as a universal element of human spirituality, and it's assumed that fasting will happen. The writers of Scripture are more

---

[68] Judges 20:26.
[69] 2 Samuel 12:16.
[70] Ezra 8:21.
[71] Matthew 4:2.
[72] Acts 13:2-3.

concerned with maintaining the spirit of prayerfulness during fasting than defining what fasting is. The Old Testament prophets warn against fasting for reasons of false piety while neglecting the true work of God, which is caring for the poor and liberating the oppressed.[73] Jesus never gives a clear indication of why we should fast, but assumes we will when he says "When you fast, don't look sad like the hypocrites who put on hungry faces to announce to the world that they're fasting."[74] Humility, sincerity, and privacy in his followers are Jesus' only concerns, and not necessarily the reasons or the outcomes of their fasting.

HOW TO FAST:

Fasting can be a way to bring your body into alignment with your spirit, especially during times of Lament or repentance. Fasting can also be a way to eliminate distractions for times of focus on the presence of God. But if you fast for either reason, remember the warnings of Jesus and the prophets – fasting must be private, and God doesn't favor fasting over our daily obligations to love our neighbors as ourselves. Just like there's no trophy in the world for the most silent meditator, there aren't any awards, even from God, for extreme periods of self-neglect. Paul wrote that severe treatment of the body looks like Godliness but actually doesn't help our spiritual development.[75] Fasting isn't an excuse to hurt yourself or to deny your body what it needs to survive. Jesus fasted for 40 days and

---

[73] Isaiah 58.
[74] Matthew 6:16.
[75] Colossians 2:23.

nights, but he also raised people from the dead and carried the sins of the whole world in his body on the cross. You're being transformed into the image of Christ, but you're not him, so be humble and reasonable about the intensity of your fasting.

HOW TO FAST FOR PURITY:

Many church traditions celebrate Lent each year, a time of fasting and self-sacrifice for the 40 days leading up to Easter. Lent parallels the ancient Jewish Passover tradition that commemorates Israel's liberation from Egypt, and also celebrates the liberation from sin and death accomplished in Christ's resurrection from the dead. The purpose of Lent is to free ourselves from the things that enslave our souls and to redirect our spiritual attention to God. These instructions work for Lent, but you don't need to wait for spring to do a Purity Fast. You can also follow this guide at any time of year to do short food fasts or longer fasts from other things.

1. IDENTIFY A SOURCE OF DISTRACTION IN YOUR LIFE AND DECIDE TO LIVE WITHOUT IT FOR A WHILE.

This isn't hard for a generation saturated by electronic media. Audio, visual, and interactive entertainment absorbs our attention and occupies huge amounts of our time. It's also highly addictive, and we find ourselves longing to sit down and watch, listen, or play as soon as we have a spare moment. Work and relationships can also be drains on our spiritual attention and resources. A fast for purity can be a rest from all of these things, and will help you reorient your spirit to the Spirit of God. If your fast involves abstaining from intimacy with your spouse, Paul teaches that they deserve a chance to set the terms and agree or disagree to your fast.[76] However you fast, be respectful and considerate of how your fast will impact others.

2. DECIDE ON A START AND END TIME FOR YOUR FAST.

It's much easier to give things up for a time than it is to simply give them up altogether. Deciding on a start and end time will also help you stay true to your commitments, since you know that your self-denial won't last forever. But don't be surprised if you find yourself free from the need to return to your habits after a period of fasting. Sometimes a break gives you the self-control you need to make necessary changes in your life.

3. DURING YOUR FAST. DEDICATE TIME FOR PRAYER AND LIFE.

The habits that consume our time occupy space in our lives. If you don't fill that space with something, it will be difficult not to return to your habits or find new ones to take their places. Set aside some of the time usually occupied by what you're abstaining from for prayer and meditation. Use the rest of the time to ask yourself what you've been neglecting in other areas of your life, and work on those things. You may simply need to allow more time to rest.

4. END YOUR FAST WITH SELF-CONTROL.

If you were able to complete your fast, don't rush back into the behavior or habit that you denied yourself. If it's something that you wish to add back into your life, do it with purpose and self-restraint. You've been set free from it, so make sure that you can enjoy it without being its slave again.

---

[76] I Corinthians 7:5.

Remember, privacy and sincerity is the primary concern of Jesus' teaching on fasting. After completing a fast, you might feel free and accomplished, but remember that this new spirituality is for you and God only. Your Father who sees in secret will reward you.

CHAPTER 7: SHARED SPIRITUALITY

Spirituality is intensely personal. Many of us feel insecure about practicing spiritual disciplines even by ourselves in private, so the thought of including others in our intimacy with God can be horrifying. Yet Christianity is a social spirituality, and group practice already plays a major role in the spiritual development of individual Christians, whether we're aware of it or not. Each worshipping community has its own traditions for group disciplines, so no specific instructions will be included here. But the Christian disciplines of Sacred Music and Sacrament are universal in our communities and are often where the spirit of prayerfulness must be first learned.

PRACTICE 11: SACRED MUSIC

Meditation is an unfamiliar concept that raises suspicions for many Christians. Closing your eyes, involving your body in your mental processes, repeating a sacred word or phrase, engaging with God emotionally, and controlling your breath seem like strange and uncomfortable ways to pray – until you realize that most Christians already do this on a weekly basis. Stranger still, we do them in public with other Christians at a scheduled time! We do all of these things, from engaging God with our emotions to breathing in rhythm, when we sing hymns and praise songs together.

Singing has always been a vital practice for the spiritual alignment of God's people. The nation of Israel responded to their liberation from Egypt with joyful singing.[77] David sang his personal struggles and victories to the Lord, and Jesus even sang one of David's songs of lament from the cross.[78] Paul and Silas sang hymns while they were in prison.[79] Paul's vision for a church "filled with the Spirit" was a joyful community speaking "to one another with Psalms, hymns, and spiritual songs, singing and making melody to the Lord with your hearts, giving thanks at all times and in everything to God the Father in the name of our Lord Jesus Christ."[80] In Revelation, God's spiritual reality as revealed to John is surprisingly full of song. The terrible action of God's kingdom

---

[77] Exodus 15.
[78] Matthew 27:46; Psalm 22.
[79] Acts 16:25.
[80] Ephesians 5:19-20.

coming into the world stops at least 14 times for angels, humans, creatures, and creation to sing epic hymns of praise to the Father and to the Lamb who was slain.[81] The Christian faith begins and ends as a spirituality of music and song.

Recent studies have shown that singing in a group has powerful effects on our minds and bodies. When we sing, our breathing is obviously synchronized, but it's been shown that our heartbeats and many important brain functions also align when we sing with others.[82] Socially, singing seems to be a potent tool for inclusion, communication, and unity in a group. A church that praises God together in song is literally uniting themselves in mind, body, and spirit, effectively following Paul's instructions to "make my joy complete by being of the same mind, having the same love, being united in one spirit, and focused on the same purpose."[83]

Of course, music has been a historical source of conflict for many Christian communities. Pastor J. Vernon McGee said, "When Satan fell, he landed in the choir loft."[84] Our human pride wants to conform the spirits of others to the image of our own spirits, not sacrifice itself so that we can all be conformed to Christ together. And of course we have aesthetic preferences. Individual spirituality is hard enough without adding the friction over music style, instrumentation, and lyrical content that comes with singing

---

[81] Revelation 4:8, 4:10-11, 5:8-10, 5:11-12, 5:13, 7:9-10, 7:11-12, 11:15, 11:17-18, 15:2-4, 16:4-5, 16:7, 19:1-2, 19:5-6.

[82] https://www.ncbi.nlm.nih.gov/pmc/articles/PMC4659897/

[83] Philippians 2:2.

[84] It was probably McGee who first said it, but the source of this quote is hard to pin down.

together. However, intimacy with God has to take priority over performance. If we remember that sacred music is a group protest against the system that rules this world, that its purpose is to glorify God and not to satisfy our preferences, and that the result is unity in mind, body, and spirit, our spiritual community should be able to experience the blessings of humbly and happily joining together in song. The spirit of prayerfulness – humility, sincerity, privacy, creativity, persistence, and receptivity – is the proper attitude for individuals seeking communion with God. It should also help us greatly as a worshipping body as we seek communion with God, together.

PRACTICE 12: SACRAMENT

The two sacred community rituals instituted by Jesus are Baptism and the "Lord's Supper" or Eucharist. Both are profound spiritual statements contained in the strikingly elemental symbols of washing and eating. Most church traditions now celebrate each occasion with a lot of regulation and ceremony. But the outward show of religious spectacle popular in our current practice runs against the spirit of simplicity intended by Jesus and the apostles. In these things too, nothing more than the spirit of prayerfulness - and of course some water, bread, and wine - is really required.

BAPTISM

Baptism is a symbol of your death and rebirth as a new creature in Christ. Symbols communicate to our subconscious in ways that words can't. Language can communicate the doctrine of the resurrection to our minds, but when we're baptized, our bodies learn and experience the resurrection too. We feel our spiritual salvation in physical experience. We understand that our new faith exists in the real world, not just the world of concepts and ideas. This also happens when we simply watch someone get baptized. When we witness a public baptism as a member of the church, the symbol of new creation is communicated to our subconscious mind. We accept the person baptized into our worshipping community, and are bound together in love and solidarity by the common experience of baptism. Again, we know this already from reading and listening to church teaching, but the act itself communicates these truths in a way that our whole selves can receive. Being baptized and witnessing baptism are spiritual experiences that are cause for reflection, celebration, and joy in the spirit of prayerfulness.

THE LORD'S SUPPER

Most Protestant churches celebrate the Lord's Supper or Eucharist with a period of serious, silent reflection on our individual sinfulness. Then we read a few verses, eat a small cracker, and drink a small cup of grape juice. The Roman Catholic tradition is similar, except that it's officiated by an endorsed professional and usually serves a little real wine. Neither practice comes close to what the Lord's Supper meant to the early church, and everything that needs to change about our church dynamics today is symbolized by our failure to celebrate together in the true spirit of the Eucharist.

The early church understood the Lord's Supper simply as "church." They got together in a home on a weeknight, prayed together, sang together, studied Scripture together, and ate together. Everything they did centered around a meal, which they called *agape* (love) feasts. At these meals, high class citizens and low class slaves talked, laughed, and shared food as equals, something totally unique in the Roman Empire. It was a time of singing, joy, and celebration, not a formal ritual. At some point during the meal, the story of Jesus' last night with his disciples was retold. Bread would be broken to symbolize his body, and wine poured as a symbol of his blood. The Christians seated around the table would all eat and drink, receiving Christ into their actual bodies as a symbolic reminder that they belonged to him, that he was in them, and that their purpose in life was to continue his work of sharing the gospel. It was a deeply spiritual experience that embodied the love and generosity of God, the humanity and sacrifice of Christ, and the continuing existence of the church that Jesus started. Christ, not a church official, was present and in charge. Christ's story was the focus, not the church's tradition or anxiety over doing everything right. Everyone was included, not just those who had performed the proper rituals, kept the moral code perfectly, or could afford to dress up. And it was probably a lot of fun.

As you experience God through your daily disciplines of prayer and meditation, ask for guidance to include others in your spirituality. Consider hosting an *agape* feast and inviting anyone who's willing to come. Look for opportunities to sing, pray, study, and eat with other Christians. Our prayer practice is private, but the full expression of our spirituality isn't meant for lonely desert mountaintops or secret rooms. One of the most consistent themes in the New Testament is that the full expression of our inner journey toward participation in God's life is our participation in the lives of our friends and neighbors – our outward love and care for each other.

CHAPTER 8: SNAKES AND TREES

When Moses came down from the mountain with the 10 Commandments, the glory of the Lord still shone from his face.[85] This was so unsettling to other people that he made a veil to hide the mark of his time with God. In Scripture, there are two interpretations of the reason for the veil. In Exodus 34, where the story is found, the people greatly feared God and sent Moses to talk to him on their behalf. When Moses returned with God's glory still lingering on his face, that same fear of God made it hard for the Israelites to communicate with Moses. He veiled his face for their benefit so that they wouldn't be afraid of him. But in the New Testament, Paul

---

[85] Exodus 34:29-35.

interprets the veil quite differently. He writes that Moses used to put the veil on his face so that "the sons of Israel wouldn't look too hard at the end of the glory that was fading away."[86] In other words, it's possible that Moses veiled his face for his own benefit because he didn't want other people to see the glory of God leaving him.

Both interpretations tell us something about the difficulty of our relationships with other people after a spiritual experience of God's presence. We have to come down from the mountain sometime, and our pride will always make it painful to transition from time with God to time with others. Just as the snake in the garden of Eden tempted the pride of Adam and Eve, there are two snakes in two trees tempting the pride of those who would deepen their experience of God through prayer. The first starts in our inner reality and moves out to cause damage to others. The second starts in our outer reality and moves inward to cause damage to us.

THE FIRST SNAKE: THE PRIDE OF MYSTICAL EXPERIENCE

Hearing God speak to you, even if it's only in silence or through your emotions, is a powerful experience. You feel special, loved, and favored by God, because you are. In fact, we all are, and Christian spirituality is an ever-growing awareness that God doesn't have favorites.[87] The cloud of worry and uncertainty lifts for a moment. You feel the peace of having your inner conflicts settled, of knowing in your soul that you belong to God, that you're saved from the power of death and that you've been adopted into God's family as a

---

[86] 2 Corinthians 3:10.
[87] Romans 2:11.

co-heir with Christ. This is what your soul has been longing for, but it's also pretty heady stuff. As you enjoy your newfound confidence with God, a thought may be whispered to you from deep within your ego: "You're not like the others. You're special. You were chosen."

That voice is the first snake in the first tree on the path of deeper prayer. The spirit of prayerfulness always says, "I am nothing without God in me." But the first snake wants your heart to proudly say, "Because of *my* practice and *my* experience, I have more God in me than everyone else. They should all recognize my spiritual superiority."

A sure sign that you've listened to the first snake is your conviction that everyone else has to immediately learn to pray as you do. You assume it's the only way God truly speaks, because it's how God has been revealed to you. This gives you the pride of superiority, of going first, of being ahead. You can dismiss the experience and insight of everyone who doesn't practice meditation, because they don't know God like you do.[88] Another sign is that you're always trying to convict other people of the same things of which the Spirit has convicted you, or trying to get other people to do what God has called you to do. You received a word of discipline because of a personal failure or weakness, and now it's your mission to convince everyone else that they struggle with the same thing. Or you received a calling to ministry or charity based on a need you observed, and now you're trying to push awareness of the need onto

---

[88] This pride doesn't just happen with prayer. A sense of spiritual superiority can come from Bible knowledge, church tradition, or moral effort as well.

other people so that they'll do all the work of obedience for you. Instead of dying to yourself, you're putting yourself in God's place as his mouthpiece.

Take this as a confession. I wouldn't recognize this snake in this tree unless I'd fallen for its temptation. But Paul directly confronts the attitude of spiritual superiority when he writes about his own mystical experience.[89] In prayer, he was taken to the "third heaven" where he heard "words no mortal can speak." But he refused to boast about the vision, boasting instead of what the power of Christ did despite and through his weaknesses. He remained humble, understanding that the spiritual gifts he was given came from God, not his own practice. His heart continued to say, "I am nothing without God in me," which shows that his spirituality was truly a process of transformation into the image of Christ.

Show grace to others who experience communion with God differently than you do. The spirit of prayerfulness is much more important than the form, and you're no judge of the spirits of others. Understand that the goal of your spiritual journey is your own transformation into Christ's image, and that it's God's work to do in you, not your work to do in yourself. Since that's true for you, remember that God has a personal interest in every other person too. God doesn't *depend* on your help to work in the lives of others, no matter your experience or your position in your religious organization. The spiritual relationship between each person and God is sacred ground, and the souls of others are not open for you to

---

[89] 2 Corinthians 12.

trespass into them. Turn the sword of conviction inward and let it kill your pride instead of using it to attack the world. When God shows you a need and calls you to act, he's calling you, not your neighbor. Respond in obedience and lead by your example of self-sacrificing service. You don't need to convince others to follow Christ your way. Do it, and if God wills it he will bring you into the company of faithful brothers and sisters whose own journeys with Christ run parallel to yours.

THE SECOND SNAKE: LONELY PROPHET SYNDROME

When you come down from the mountain of new prayer experience, glowing and inspired, you might be surprised to see good people from your Christian tradition withdraw from you. The more you tell them about your new practices or experience, the more they'll doubt your faithfulness to God or your commitment to the Bible. All you're trying to tell them is that you feel a more intimate connection with the God of the Bible through prayer. This should be a cause for celebration, not a source of fear. But something about the way you've experienced communion with God worries them. Their concern for you will make it impossible for them to hear what you're saying when you explain scary things like prayer beads and meditation. They'll think you've been influenced by some kind of New Age heresy from outside the bounds of the Christian faith, or led astray by that other church that's your church's sworn enemy. In the moment when you feel the closest to God, you might start to notice a painful distance growing between you and your community of faith.

As that distance grows, the voice of the second snake will whisper: "You're all alone now. There's no one else like you. They'll never accept you again. Maybe they're right about you. Are you really closer to God, or have you been fooled?"

The prophet Elijah knew the voice of the second snake. From a cave in the wilderness he prayed, "I have served the Lord God Almighty with faithfulness. But all the rest of your people have broken their covenant with you... I am the only one left, and now they are trying to kill me, too."[90]

You'll know that you've listened to the second snake when you feel like your family and faith community have abandoned you or put you on trial. You'll start to avoid them, or you'll find yourself desperately defending unimportant secondary things like prayer beads and sitting in silence. You'll try harder and harder to repeat the spiritual experiences that first helped you experience the presence of God, always trying to prove to yourself that it wasn't just "in your head." You'll beg God to show himself to you more clearly than ever to prove everyone wrong about you. But instead of inner silence and connection with God, your anxious mind will replay the criticism of your loved ones on a loop that never ends. The first snake wants to flatter your pride until you're using your spiritual experience to gain authority over others. The second snake wants to wound your pride until you're ashamed of your spiritual experience or desperately defending it to your community of faith. In both states, the snake has brought separation to your relationships

---

[90] 1 Kings 19:10.

and has you using your prayer practice for something other than communion with God. In both states, you've abandoned the commandments to love God with your heart, soul, mind, and strength and to love your neighbor as yourself. In both states, you're living as an image of your pride and not as the image of Christ.

SO, WHAT TO DO?

The Christian answer to everything is self-sacrifice in the image of Christ. Jesus emptied himself of his divine nature to become a person, for your sake. Jesus died at the hands of the people he came to serve, for your sake. Jesus washed Judas' feet, asked forgiveness for the Roman soldiers who crucified him, and forgave Peter after he denied him three times. That same Peter wrote this:

> *"But if you endure when you suffer for doing good, this is a gracious thing in the sight of God. This is what you were called for, because Christ suffered for you. He left you an example so that you might follow in his steps. He committed no sin and used no deceitful words. When he was hated, he did not hate in return; he did not threaten when he suffered, but always entrusted himself to the one who judges rightly. He took our sins on himself in his body on the cross so that we can die to sin and live to righteousness. You have been healed by his wounds. You were straying like sheep, but have now returned to the Shepherd and Caretaker of your souls."[91]*

Follow Jesus' example and maintain the spirit of prayerfulness in the face of trouble. Stay humble, sincere, private, creative, persistent, and receptive. "Love bears all things, believes all things, hopes all things, endures all things."[92] Remain in the love of Christ. Love

---

[91] 1 Peter 2:20-25.

everyone as he has loved you. Love the Lord your God with all your heart, soul, mind, and strength. Love your neighbor as yourself. And pray for God's help to die well.

[92] 1 Corinthians 13:7.

A FINAL WORD: THE TEMPLE AND THE WIND

In John 2, Jesus cleanses the Jerusalem temple with a whip. He then makes his famous challenge: "Tear down this temple and I will rebuild it in 3 days." The religious officials respond by doubting Jesus' ability to complete such an ambitious construction project, but John notes that Jesus was actually talking about replacing the temple with his body.[93] Jesus' body, which was killed and resurrected after three days, is God's replacement for the temple - the place the presence of the Holy Spirit calls home. And, according to Paul, through Christ *your* body is God's temple too.[94]

---

[93] John 2:21.
[94] 1 Corinthians 6:19.

In the following chapter, John tells the story of Jesus' meeting with a religious official named Nicodemus. When Nicodemus doesn't understand a metaphor about being born again, Jesus challenges him to rise above the need to have everything understood or under control: "The wind blows wherever it wants. You can hear it, but you can't see where it comes from or where it goes. That's how it is with everyone who is born of the Spirit."[95] The temple is replaced with the simple existence of our human bodies. Logical explanations are replaced with unpredictable wind. The Spirit calls us away from the safety of architecture and understanding, out into the wild and uncontrollable world of God's presence.

As you move into deeper prayer through these practices, there will be times when you're inspired, comfortable, and settled in the love of God. You'll feel joyful, like you've found your center, solid ground, your home, and your true self. But the feeling won't last forever. Your presence to the presence of God comes and goes as your circumstances and relationships change and as you change and grow as a person. In these times of transition and uncertainty it can feel like you're losing your intimacy with God. You might return to prayer practices that once brought you immediate joy and peace, only to find them difficult, frustrating, and unrewarding. Confidence in your ability to encounter God through prayer disappears like mist. You feel dry, cold, dark, and abandoned.

The bittersweet reality is that times of spiritual darkness have been the common experience of all serious Christian mystics since

---

[95] John 3:8.

the time of Jesus. Our prayer practices can quickly turn into just another temple for God that we visit on our own terms and our own schedule. We easily fall into the delusion that God responds to our mystical arts and forget that our lives of prayer are actually responses to God in the first place. Thankfully, the living God always resists our attempts to domesticate or tame him, and often does so by withdrawing from us and our prayer practices. This is painful, but it's for our good. God does not want us to live in the delusion that we can control or manipulate him. God relates to us as he is, free and wild and unpredictable, and he takes action to remind us of who he is when we forget. It can feel like trying to catch up to the wind, but as Jesus said, that's just how life goes when you're born of the Spirit.

So change, adapt, wonder, evolve, grow, love, learn and try new things! God is not contained by temples, but freely and incredibly dwells in our bodies and in the winds of growth and change. You'll never *catch* the wind, so learn to listen to it instead. All you really need to do is show up and be present.

BENEDICTION

May you find God and lose him often,

May you lose your life to find yourself.

May you come to true knowledge,

May you forget all you know and be captivated by mystery.

May times of rest heal you,

May times of wilderness bring you growth,

And may your seasons of peace and trial never be more than you can bear.

Above all, may the same God who said "Let there be light"

Shine the light of his glory into your heart,

So that the light of Christ will shine from your heart

And bring the light of love into your world.

To the Father who makes you, the Son who saves you, and the Spirit who dwells in you,

May your spirit always say:

AMEN.

APPENDIX 1: THE PSALMS BY TYPE

The German scholar of the Old Testament Herman Gunkel pioneered the division of the Psalms by genre. In the personal devotional life, it can be helpful to know which Psalms speak to different human experiences so that we can pray biblically in response to present situations. Although some Psalms are hard to classify, here's a basic overview of Gunkel's genres and the Psalms that seem to fit into them.[96]

HYMNS – PRAISE TO GOD.

> Psalms 8, 19, 29, 33, 65, 67, 68, 96, 98, 100, 103, 104, 105, 111, 113, 114, 117, 135, 136, 139, 145, 146, 147, 148, 149, 150.

SONGS OF ZION – PRAISE OF GOD'S HOLY CITY.

> Psalms 46, 48, 76, 84, 87, 122.

SONGS OF GOD'S ROYALTY/ENTHRONEMENT – PRAISE TO GOD THE KING.

> Psalms 2, 18, 20, 21, 45, 47, 72, 89, 93, 96, 97, 99, 101, 110, 132, 144.

LAMENT PSALMS – SONGS OF PROTEST AND COMPLAINT.

COMMUNITY LAMENTS

> Psalms 44, 58, 60, 74, 79, 80, 83, 106, 125.

---

[96] This overview is adapted from the work of Tyler F. Williams, Assistant Professor of Theology at The King's University College in Edmonton, Alberta. http://biblical-studies.ca/pdfs/Gunkel_Classification_of_the_Psalms.pdf

INDIVIDUAL LAMENTS

> Psalms 3, 5, 6, 7, 13, 17, 22, 25, 26, 27, 28, 31, 35, 38, 39, 42, 43, 54, 55, 56, 57, 59, 61, 63, 64, 69, 70, 71, 86, 88, 102, 109, 120, 130, 140, 141, 142, 143.

CONFESSION PSALMS – SONGS OF INDIVIDUAL OR COMMUNITY REPENTANCE.

> Psalms 51, 78, 81, 106, 130.

CURSING PSALMS – SONGS ASKING FOR GOD'S JUDGMENT ON ENEMIES.[97]

> Psalms 35, 69, 83, 88, 109, 137, 140.

TRUST PSALMS – SONGS DECLARING FAITH IN GOD.

> Psalms 4, 11, 16, 23, 27, 62, 125, 131.

THANKSGIVING PSALMS – SONGS OF INDIVIDUAL AND COMMUNITY GRATITUDE.

> Psalms 18, 30, 32, 34, 40, 41, 66, 67, 92, 100, 107, 116, 118, 124, 129, 138.

TEACHING PSALMS – SONGS OF WISDOM.

> Psalms 1, 37, 49, 73, 91, 112, 127, 128, 133.

MISCELLANEOUS PSALMS

> Psalms 9, 10, 12, 36, 50, 52, 75, 77, 82, 90, 94, 108, 119, 123, and 137 have their own unique styles or represent a mix of other styles.
>
> Psalms 15, 20, 24, 14/53, 66, 81, 82, 85, 95, 107, 115, 118, 121, 126, 132, and 134 were probably used in a reading-

---

[97] Jesus teaches us not to hate our enemies but to pray for them. Yet if we're honest, we often find ourselves hating and cursing others in our hearts. The Cursing Psalms can help us exaggerate those feelings in prayer, drawing them out before God so that we can confess them and deal with them under his guidance.

response style of worship.

Psalms 78, 105, and 106 praise God based on Israel's history.

Psalm 122 is a song for a pilgrimage.

APPENDIX 2: RESOURCES & FURTHER READING

It would be impossible to list all of the sources that went into preparing this little book. Since my goal is to provide guidance for your further study, here are 12 resources that have helped shape my spirituality, are helpful for further exploration of the dynamics of prayer, and are written in a way that's accessible for non-professional Christian readers:

Ahlberg Calhoun, Adele. *Spiritual Disciplines Handbook: Practices That Transform Us.* IVP Books, 2015.

Brueggemann, Walter. *Praying the Psalms: Engaging Scripture and the Life of the Spirit.* Wipf and Stock Publishers, 2007.

Chan, Francis. *Forgotten God: Reversing Our Tragic Neglect of the Holy Spirit.* David C. Cook, 2009.

Contemplative Outreach Ltd. "Centering Prayer" Mobile App. Available from www.contemplativeoutreach.org. 2016.

Jethani, Skye. *With: Reimagining the Way You Relate To God.* Thomas Nelson, 2011.

ed. Mursell, Gordon. *The Story of Christian Spirituality: Two Thousand Years, From East to West.* Minneapolis: Fortress Press, 2001.

Newell, J.P. *Listening for the Heartbeat of God: A Celtic Spirituality.* Paulist Press, 1997.

Peterson, Eugene. *Reversed Thunder: The Revelation of John and the Praying Imagination.* HarperOne, 1991.

Rohr, Richard. *The Naked Now: Learning to See as the Mystics See.* The Crossroad Publishing Company, 2009.

Renovare Resources. *The Life With God Bible.* HarperOne, 2009.

Tozer, A.W. *The Pursuit of God.* Christian Publications, 1948.

Vincent, Kristen E. *A Bead And A Prayer: A Beginner's Guide to Protestant Prayer Beads.* Upper Room, 2013.

ABOUT THE AUTHOR

Jon, his wife Belen, and their children live in the tropical and culturally diverse Rio Grande Valley of Texas. As a sunny and culturally diverse family, this suits them just fine. They have been student ministers for 10 years and love it. Jon is also nearly finished with a MA in Religion from Logsdon Theological Seminary and plans to continue working in the area of accessible Christian spirituality. If you would like to contact him or check out the very early stages of some of his other work, go to www.mikroi.org or send an e-mail to jesusliteracy@gmail.com.

Thank you for reading, and may the love of God always shine on you!

98395585R00063

Made in the USA
Columbia, SC
24 June 2018